Don't Kiss Them Good-bye

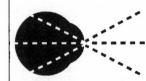

This Large Print Book carries the
Seal of Approval of N.A.V.H.

Don't Kiss Them Good-bye

Allison DuBois

Thorndike Press • Waterville, Maine

Published in 2005 by arrangement with
Simon & Schuster, Inc.

Thorndike Press® Large Print Core.

The tree indicium is a trademark of Thorndike Press.

The text of this Large Print edition is unabridged.
Other aspects of the book may vary from the original edition.

Set in 16 pt. Plantin by Elena Picard.

Printed in the United States on permanent paper.

Library of Congress Cataloging-in-Publication Data

DuBois, Allison.
    Don't kiss them good-bye / by Allison DuBois.
      p. cm.
    ISBN 0-7862-7828-5 (lg. print : hc : alk. paper)
    1. DuBois, Allison. 2. Mediums — United States —
Biography. 3. Large type books. I. Title.
    BF1283.D82A3 2005b
    133.9′1′092—dc22   2005010859

This book is dedicated to fathers. I have recently realized just how precious fathers can be. Four extraordinary men I was fortunate enough to have known passed away in 2002:

My father, Mike Gomez, whom I adored and will miss until the day I die. He wasn't a typical dad. He started giving me facials at the age of nine so that I could avoid wrinkles when I was older. Nice try, Dad! You had to love him. He lived to be sixty-seven, but inside, he was just a tenacious child. I know that he will dance among the stars forever with all the beautiful ladies. Nobody laughed or lived quite like my dad.

My good friend Randy passed away seven weeks after my dad. He was the Seafood King and my favorite skeptic. Randy made everything into an event for all to enjoy. Like my dad, he died of a heart attack, except he was only forty-nine years old. He leaves the world with three amazing kids and a wife with whom he shared his vibrant spirit.

My sarcastically funny great-uncle Don, a former sheriff and a pilot in World War II. He made it to eighty and took his final flight that January.

Russ Serzen, a former New York Yankee and all-around great dad. I only knew him briefly but he left unexpectedly from Creutzfeldt-Jakob disease (a fatal brain disease). He left a lasting impression on me. He was to be admired.

All of these men lived life large and made no apologies for who they were. They were all inspirations, and they were all dads.

Acknowledgments

Joe: You are the man who has held my hand through all the bumps in the night. You have my undying adoration. Thank you for understanding me.

My girls: You have enabled me to understand why parents can't let go when they lose a child. I will be with you always.

Mom: Thank you for some of my best childhood memories. I love you.

Dad: I love you. Thank you for teaching me to smile in the face of adversity.

Grandpa Joe: Even though you are on the other side, we are . . . connected. You are one of the most honorable men ever.

Uncle Joe and Aunt Linda: Thank you for always making me feel I belong.

Grandma Jenee: Thank you for sharing my gift and helping make me who I am. I love you.

Mary Frances: You comfort me. Thank you for gracing my life.

Jim: Thank you for staying with us and for your guidance.

Wendy: Thank you for being my sounding board. You're a good friend.

Stacey: Thank you for your friendship and the many times you made me laugh. When I couldn't pick myself up you gave me your strength. You are family.

Christina: You are one of a kind and will remain a friend of mine for life. Thank you for knowing me as "Allison" and all of the goofy moments that we have shared.

Christy, my friend who helped me in the writing of my book: You remind me how little attention I paid in college English. Your contribution is infinite. Thank you! You are an exceptional woman.

Trevor: I loved you before you were ever born.

Dr. Gary Schwartz: You are an exceptionally intelligent man who is courageous enough to be a pioneer in his field. I admire your foresight. Thank you for sharing my journey.

Kelsey: I've never met a human being with such presence. You physically knocked me over when you stood beside me. You're an extraordinary man with many wonderful gifts.

8

Susy: You're an amazing teacher. Walk with me always.

Little Michael: Remember you are always a part of us. I love you!

My brother Michael: You mean the world to me.

Shari: You helped raise me. Thank you. Cheers!

Domini: I miss you. Don't forget to visit me regularly.

Laurie Campbell: The medium that other mediums consult. Thank you for raising the bar and for being my friend. Your dad is very proud!

Charlie and Susie Shaughnessy: Thank you for your valuable words of wisdom. You are two special people. If I can ever be of service to you, just say the word.

Jerry Conser: You not only helped me in the writing of my book, you were the only person who knew there was something different about me as a child. You are a special man, and I thank you.

Glenn Gordon Caron: Nobody does it better. To sum your talent up in one word would be impossible. You're that good. I can never thank you enough for capturing me.

Gary Hart: Thank you for remembering me. I'll always remember you.

Patricia: You're an enigma! Thank you for never wavering from who you are.

"Chief": I will always look up to you. A legal genius *and* good-looking — how did you manage that? Hee-hee!

Patty: You are the woman I had hoped to grow up to be. You are so good at putting those bad guys away. You are one of my closest friends. Thanks for being the maverick that you are.

Connie: You're the best, never to be underestimated. Thank you for your guidance.

Dr. Julie Beischel: You are an extraordinary scientist unafraid of the possibilities. Thank you.

Bert Sass: Thank you for taking me seriously.

Jim Manley: Keep breaking those glass ceilings.

Missing Children: We will never stop looking for you . . . ever.

Maggie, Carol, Susan, Sylvia, Maddy, Rami, Suzy, Barb: You are all special.

Grammnet: Thank you for all your hard work.

Steve Stark: My admiration for you is a drop in the bucket.

Chris Maul: You will grow into the best in the business.

Julie Mondimore: Congrats on your baby boy. He is blessed to have you as a mother.

Paramount: Thank you for being the best!

Jennifer Solari: Your dad is truly proud of his little girl.

NBC: You are the network I wanted the most. Thank you to everyone for being top-notch.

Cathryn Boxberger: You are a woman of many facets. Thank you for being exceptional.

Jeff Zucker: I am honored to know you and your talent.

Kevin Riley: Thank you for appreciating me and being a great man of vision.

Chris Conti: Drive carefully! Thank you for seeing me for who I am. You are a great man.

Simon & Schuster: You have my gratitude for caring so much.

Nancy Hancock: You are not only a phenomenal woman, you are the one who found me.

Ellen Silberman: Genius! Thank you for working your magic.

A special thank-you to **all the people mentioned in my book.** You have helped me to grow.

My guides: Thank you for never steering me wrong and for sharing my mischievous sense of humor.

Contents

Foreword

Gary E. Schwartz, Ph.D.
Human Energy Systems Laboratory
University of Arizona

Sometimes people not only have gifts but are themselves gifts. Allison DuBois is not only a gifted psychic medium, she is an extraordinary gift to others. She gifts not only her husband, children, family, and friends but also the clients who call her for help and counsel in her role as an evidence-based psychic medium.

In my role as an evidence-based scientist investigating the possibility of survival of consciousness, I have witnessed Allison do things that I would have thought, just a few years ago, must be impossible. Allison achieves the seemingly impossible with gentleness, ease, kindness, and understanding that bring a smile to one's face and joy to one's heart.

Prior to meeting Allison, I had conducted research with a group of remarkably gifted mediums. In my book *The Afterlife Experiments: Breakthrough Scientific Evidence of Life*

After Death, I discuss a series of experiments with John Edward of *Crossing Over*, George Anderson, Suzanne Northrop, Laurie Campbell, and Anne Geymen — individuals I have come to describe as Michael Jordans of mediumship. After working with Allison, it became clear to me that she was the new member of this dream team of mediums.

I must confess that Allison holds a special place in my heart. The reason is that I first met her, coincidentally, just two days after the passing of my adopted grandmother, the late Susy Smith, who died unexpectedly from a massive heart attack. The truth is, I loved Susy, and I was not prepared for her sudden passing.

Susy was eighty-nine years old, the author of thirty books on parapsychology and survival of consciousness after death, and a successful participant in some of our early research on mediumship in the Human Energy Systems Laboratory at the University of Arizona. She was featured in *The Afterlife Experiments*. Susy devoted the last forty-five years of her life to the question "Is the afterlife real?" In fact, she could not wait to die so that she could prove, scientifically, that she was still here.

When Susy died, my role as a scientist expanded greatly. I was no longer just the senior experimenter. I became a research "sitter" (someone who wants to learn about the fortunes of a deceased loved one).

As Allison recounts in her last chapter, "Science and the Other Side," at our first meeting, I asked her whether she could receive any information about a person close to me who had died recently. I did not give any information about age, sex, or relationship, and I provided virtually no feedback — visual or verbal — as Allison attempted to demonstrate her skills in the laboratory.

Allison received meaningful and evidential information about Susy, including the cause of her passing (heart attack), her dreams for her future in the afterlife (for example, her desire be with her little deceased dog, Junior), and most important, a message for me about her new freedom from physical disability. Allison said, and I paraphrase, "The deceased is telling me, over and over, that I must share the following: I don't walk alone." Why are these four words important? Because Susy was confined to a wheelchair for the last ten years of her life. In fact, Susy told me many times of her desire to go dancing in the afterlife once she had finally shed her painful physical body.

According to many sessions of evidence provided by Allison, Susy is alive and well on the other side. As I write these words, our research continues, spanning not only three generations — Susy, Gary (me), and Allison — but two sides of the living energy universe: here and there. For me what is most important is that Allison is committed to truth. Allison knows that her personal integrity, the integrity of the Human Energy Systems Laboratory, and the integrity of the work she represents, require absolute honesty with humility.

Allison writes as she is: clear, warm, intelligent, and lighthearted. May this book inspire your hopes and dreams as it has mine. Allison, we thank you for this gift of gifts.

GARY E. SCHWARTZ, Ph.D., is professor of psychology, medicine, neurology, psychiatry, and surgery, and director of the Human Energy Systems Laboratory at the University of Arizona. He received his Ph.D. in personality psychology from Harvard University in 1971. After teaching at Harvard for five years, he became professor of psychology and psychiatry at Yale University, director of the Yale Psychophysiology Center, and co-director of the Yale Behavioral Medicine Clinic. He moved to Arizona in 1988.

He has co-edited eleven academic books; published more than four hundred scientific papers, including six in the journal *Science*; and co-written two books, *The Living Energy Universe* and *The Afterlife Experiments*. His current research on energy medicine and survival of consciousness has been featured in television, radio, newspapers, and magazines. His television appearances include the HBO documentaries *Life After Life* and *America Undercover* and the A&E special *Beyond Death*; and on Discovery, *Dateline*, *Nightline*, and *Good Morning America*.

Introduction

For those of you familiar with the hit television series *Medium* you probably already know that it's based on my real experiences. For those of you unfamiliar with the show, I encourage you to tune in and explore life after death. *Don't Kiss Them Good-bye* elaborates on my life minus the great television writers. It is my way of sharing with you how I'm affected by being a medium. Perhaps you are intrigued by my being able to see and feel events that not all people can. Perhaps learning about mediums will raise questions for you about your own life. Maybe you're one of many who knows your loved ones are still around and you want to strengthen your connections with them. I invite you to join me on this adventure through my life so that you can better understand how the events in my life have shaped who I am. I will give you a glimpse of what life can be after death. I also will talk to you about how to stay connected to those who matter to you most. May this book inspire you as so many have inspired me.

In this book, I share my own childhood experiences in order to connect and relate to young mediums who have questions and doubts about their gifts. I hope that my experiences can help show how a child with the gift might feel or view things. I also hope it illustrates how we, as people who love the gifted young, can help them to understand and embrace their abilities. Figuring out our gifts in life is part of our journey to becoming enlightened human beings. I want the people reading my book to have real insight into the life of a person with special abilities. I want you to better understand where psychics and mediums come from and what kinds of potential we have. Being able to relate to or think about the unknown is half the battle of expanding your spiritual beliefs. Having the opportunity to experience it personally is the other half.

✦ *About Me*

I am a medium and profiler. This means I can predict future events, I can get into a person's mind, I can detect health problems in people, and I can communicate with the dead. Yes, I see dead people.

I have often wished that someone would come up with a better word than "psychic" to describe people like me. Between all the con artists out there and the gypsy and witch stereotypes, the word has been forever tainted. Call it what you want; I have what I refer to as the gift.

I was brought into this world in the usual way on January 24, 1972, in Phoenix, Arizona. I'm old enough to have learned my craft and young enough to challenge it. I have one older brother, Michael, who teased me often. My parents divorced when I was a baby, but I grew up knowing they both loved me.

Even when I was little I knew that I wasn't a typical kid. Besides my encounter with my great-grandpa after his funeral (which I discuss in the chapter "A Little Girl Meets the Other Side"), there were many other significant signs of things to come.

I identified with characters who had special gifts. Whether it was Tabitha on *Bewitched* or Tia in *Escape to Witch Mountain*, I knew they were different, like me. I was sure they could relate to my feelings of being an oddity, misunderstood by adults. As I was careful about what information I shared with people, I understood why the characters on TV or in the movies hid their abilities.

My identification with these characters went beyond a child's imagination and the desire to be Wonder Woman or Superman. When I was around ten years old, I was told repeatedly (by those I have come to know as my guides) that I was unique. They told me that when I was older I would affect people in a profound way. It was hard then for me to imagine that I could do something that important someday.

I received visits from my guides on and off throughout my childhood and teenage years. I wasn't sure who those voices were, but I knew the source was good and that it was coming from upstairs. I could feel the energy of the visitor and, although I was not frightened, I was more afraid that I would not be able to live up to their expectations of me.

I couldn't help but think Why me? I look average, and my parents are divorced. I found church boring. My mom made me go with her every Sunday and I resented it. I preferred to talk to heaven personally when I was alone. I felt very connected to a higher power and I was sensitive to others' feelings about it. But it seemed that all the adults at church sang about one thing and then practiced another. It didn't make sense to me, but if I mentioned this I was scolded.

I filled my room with stuffed animals and dolls, but mine served a defensive purpose. I lined them up on shelves, on the floor, everywhere, positioned to fill space and form a barrier between me and the unknown. Since I could feel many variations of energy around me and sometimes I saw apparitions, my stuffed animals filled the physical void where I knew the energy existed. The toys also helped calm my nerves. I had created in my mind an explanation for the energy I felt. I was no longer looking at empty space and feeling as though an unknown energy occupied it. My toys now filled the space. Children, like adults, learn to deal with complicated circumstances in a way that creates comfort for them.

I spent my youth trying to convince myself that I was normal. I was a competitive roller skater for several years in the early eighties. Journey, REO Speedwagon, and The Go-Go's provided the background music for my childhood. The people at the rink were also quite memorable, with their big perms, leg warmers, and lights on their skate wheels. I sat for hours watching people skate around faster and faster, until they began to blur into circles of light. I watched them intently, as if I were looking for something inside each person to become visible.

I enjoyed the all-or-nothing stakes of winning competitions. Figures, dance, freestyle skating — I did them all. I especially loved those rare occasions when the boys and girls were allowed to compete against one another. I enjoyed beating the boys the most.

Skating also provided an escape from the conflict at home between my mom and stepdad. When I was twelve, my mom and the man that I had called dad for ten years dissolved their marriage. I saw him with his new family a year later. He didn't see me and I never saw him again.

My mom remarried a year or two later, and I didn't fit into the new arrangement. I was on my own just one month before my sixteenth birthday. I lived in an apartment with a high school friend named Domini. I remember kicking back with a beer and thinking how ludicrous it was that I had once told my sixth grade teacher that I aspired to go to Harvard. Ridiculous! I thought. At this rate I wouldn't even be going to a community college!

My teenage years were painful and lonely. People were all around me, but I felt as alone as anyone could be. I also felt as if I sometimes attracted people who had bad energy. I always worry about young people who stand out in crowds because they have an inner light that shines through. I heard this often as a young person and now I understand it. Dark entities are naturally attracted to light and will try to manipulate it. A dark entity can see a light entity from a mile away. Unfortunately, it's typically harder for light entities to spot dark ones, but with experience they can learn to recognize and avoid them.

Have you ever looked at a recent picture of someone close to you and compared it to one from the past? There is a light that flickers in a young person's eyes that is often extinguished as he ages. The trick is to make sure your light remains strong and bright. It's a reflection of your soul. Never let it be extinguished. I have met seventy-year-old men and women who have the essence of people in their early twenties. I am determined to always retain my mischievous inner youth.

The night I met my husband he swears there was a light shining down on me. Joe says he couldn't resist knowing what I was about. I thought he was just an irritating guy with a pickup line. Joe has helped to make me a better person. He has taught me many lessons that I wouldn't have held still long enough to hear from anyone else. The most important thing he taught me is that there are people who are true to their word, people who will always be there. He has taught me to trust.

Another lesson Joe taught me was math and that it wasn't too late to apply it to my dream of going to college. Against all the odds I did graduate from college. I received a B.A. in political science with a minor in history from Arizona State University. Even though I had grown up around all kinds of people who were going nowhere fast, a part of me had always known that somehow, some way, I would earn a college degree. I guess I am just one of those lucky people for whom things always work out. I see myself as being constantly pushed back onto the right path by a force greater than me. I am thankful.

While sitting in class at ASU, feeling sorry for myself, I met a girl in a wheelchair. She was blind and had a Seeing Eye dog, but I never heard her complain, not once! I got over feeling sorry for myself really quickly. Life is a series of learning important lessons.

You have to pay attention in class. Thinking of her helps me remember there's always someone who has it harder than I do.

Overall, my twenties were rich and exciting. I made mistakes, met Joe, graduated from college, experienced motherhood, interned at the homicide bureau, produced a safety video, and prepared myself to start over again with a new story. I don't know how I ended up with such a colorful, remarkable life, but I am thankful for all I have done and all that I have.

Now that you know my background and what I do, I encourage you to use the rest of my book to think about your own experiences.

Please remember that mediums serve people both living and dead. We bridge the gap. If you have ever questioned whether there is an afterlife, I hope this book will help you to see that indeed there is a whole world on the other side.

Chapter 1

My Way

I stared out the window that overlooked my backyard. I looked up at the stars in the sky, then back down to my girls' play set.

"Dad, where are you?"

I studied every part of my backyard.

"I can see everyone else; why not you? I can't see what you look like now! I *need* to see you."

I sobbed as though I could expel the heartache from my body through my tears. But no matter how hard I cried, the excruciating pain refused to leave.

I collapsed onto my couch and observed the house that I had moved into less than four weeks ago. The house I had moved into to be closer to my dad. But my dad would never get to walk through my front door, because he had died suddenly less than twenty-four hours ago.

Two days earlier I had spoken with my neighbor Alison, whom I had just met when we moved in. Her father had unexpectedly been diagnosed with an advanced brain disease, and his prognosis wasn't good. He was a wonderful man and I had been privileged to meet him on one occasion.

I had told her, "I know it's hard to see any gifts in your dad's condition but let me point out one. I counsel many people who are devastated because they never got to say good-bye. You have been given an opportunity to hold your dad, to sit with him, and when the time comes to say good-bye to him. Say and do whatever you need to now in order to be okay with his final moments. One thing that I cannot do as a medium is to hold those lost to me. I can somewhat touch them but not hold them. It's not the same. See the gift."

Later Alison and I would recognize the significance of our new friendship.

My father's death came at the end of a fun weekend. On September 20, 2002, I traveled to California for my cousin Vanessa's wedding. I was happy to be there with my husband, Joe; we needed a break. During the ceremony some unusual disturbances were taking place. I snickered and squeezed Joe's hand.

I knew that my dad's sister, my aunt Olivia, who had passed six years earlier, was making her presence known. I'd never doubted she would be there; I'd only wondered how she'd make her presence known. After the wedding we followed my cousin Mark's fiancée to the reception; she missed our exit and we ended up on a small road trip. It made us a little late, but when we arrived we were ready for a good time.

The timing of our arrival would later seem very important. We walked into the ballroom and I heard a familiar song. That moment will stay in my mind forever. The mariachis were playing "My Way." First of all, I've never heard that song played at a wedding, because it's hardly about unity. Second, mariachis don't typically play that song, because it's in English. I whirled around and I looked at Joe and my cousin Mark.

Oh my gosh! That's so strange — that's what I'm going to play someday at Dad's funeral!

"My Way" is a perfect song for my dad, not only because he was a free spirit but because he had an air of Rat Pack coolness about him. He had been a professional ballroom dancer for decades, and we used to listen to Frank Sinatra together. He wore a big diamond pinky ring, and when I was seventeen I began wearing my own as a way of connecting to my dad. Everything he did, he did with style.

Two years earlier, I had made a prediction. One day after having lunch with my dad, I came home and told my husband that I had a strong feeling my dad was going to die at age sixty-seven from a massive heart attack. Since then I had been on a crusade to prevent it. I shared my prediction with a few friends and family members. My friend Stacey and I had already gone to the mall and picked up a Sinatra CD with "My Way" on it. I told her I'd need it for my dad's funeral. I was simultaneously planning his funeral and trying to prevent it. My dad promised he'd go have his heart checked out, and he did, several times; the doctors said all was well.

I snapped back to the reception, and as the song ended I felt sick to my stomach.

"Shake it off. Dad is fine," I said to myself as I prayed it true. I had sent him to every heart institute in our area. He exercised regularly and ate right. He listened to me. Intervention, right?

It was Friday, and I had just talked to Dad the night before. I'd planned to call on Sunday when I got home. He was coming over for lunch the following Saturday. I missed my dad the whole time I was gone. I'd moved to central Phoenix from Gilbert, Arizona, so that we could spend more time together. I was eager to see him more often. I had been in Phoenix for only three weeks, and I was still unpacking.

Sunday morning, we were hanging out with my cousin Mark and my friend Laurie, waiting until we had to catch our flight home in a few hours. The phone rang and Joe answered it. After listening briefly, he looked at me and said, "Allison, your dad died."

I felt as if all the breath had been sucked out of my body.

"You mean my grandma? Dad couldn't be gone!"

The look on Joe's face told me he was. My heart shattered instantly. I could not think straight.

I was so angry with God: "You can't take my dad! I live with ridicule and doubt from others and I still do what I'm asked to do. I have done everything you've asked of me without hesitation, but a condition was that you not take my father!"

I was only thirty years old, with no father. My daughters would have no grandfather; two of them would be too young to re-member him clearly. I counsel others on grief, and I could not give myself peace of mind. I was instantly empty. I had *nothing* left to give.

As I flew home, I watched people go on with their lives. I wanted to say, "Stop! My father has died and everything must stop!"

But it doesn't work that way. I know that. I was being irrational, but I couldn't help myself. As I grappled with my pain, I realized that I was Dad's next of kin and I had a funeral to plan.

Death is funny in that it brings out the best and the worst in people. It casts light on the truth and makes life blindingly clear. The reality was starting to set in. I went to pick up the personal items he'd been wearing, and I slipped his pinky ring onto my finger next to my own pinky ring, where it will always stay. I had no sense of time, of hunger, or of any of life's normal routines. Everything had all smeared together into an ugly, distorted mess. I told my husband that I didn't want to sleep because every night that I slept was one more day since Dad's last breath. I didn't want Dad to become a distant memory. I didn't know how to function, and I was frustrated because I couldn't feel him as I do others who have passed.

At his funeral I saw my cousin Mike, my dad's namesake, and we embraced. Mike handed me the most amazing picture. It was of my dad and Mike's dad with their arms around each other at Mike's wedding twenty years ago. They had the most brilliant smiles on their faces and were obviously having a great time. Mike's dad had passed away ten years earlier. I was so grateful for the picture. I extended my hand to Mike and placed my dad's gold watch in his hand. It had been his favorite; "Mike" was engraved on the back, and he wore it every day.

"My dad would want you to have this," I said.

Mike smiled. "Allison, my dad engraved this watch for your dad. I recognize his work."

I believe that Mike and I were prompted by our dads, so that each of us would bring a token of their love and hand it off to the child who missed a father. The watch gave my cousin not only love from my dad but a sign from his dad. The picture gave me a sense of happiness I thought I'd never feel again, as well as the gift of a visual of how he looks on the other side. I couldn't yet reach my dad, but he reached me.

Then I suddenly felt angry. "I am standing at my father's funeral!"

I looked up at the stained-glass ceiling of the church, and once again I railed at God: "How could you take him like this? Why should I ever listen to you again?"

I heard a soft female voice say, "You were given the gift of *two years* to say good-bye."

The voice was right. I had been given two years! Even though I wasn't with my father at the moment of his passing, I had been saying good-bye every time I saw or spoke with him. I had been saying good-bye with my every word and action for two years, and I knew it. I had known my father's days were numbered since the day I received his age and cause of passing.

It had been a blessing and a curse at once. I reflected upon my last conversation with Dad. I had told him, "Hold on, Dad, I'll help you when I get back. Don't you leave me; I still need you."

He didn't answer me, so I told him I loved him and hung up. It's interesting that I couldn't separate the medium in me from the daughter. My words had clearly been acknowledging loss. I just wouldn't see it, because this time I just had to be wrong.

It dawned on me that if I'd had a choice I never would have let him go. So God decides when it's time for our souls to move forward, when it's time to leave this life. None of us would simply relinquish our loved ones, or ourselves for that matter: "Okay, God take 'em away! Good-bye!" No, I don't see that happening.

Initially, I was unable to make contact with my father because I was blocked by my own pain, but eventually he reached me. The week after he passed away, I received phone calls from two of my dad's dance students. The calls were independent of each other and neither student knew that I am a medium. I know my father didn't tell them. His response to learning about my ability had been "Well, don't tell anyone!"

They both shared with me that they had a dream in which they saw my father. They said he looked really good and happy. In both dreams they had conversations with him and he told them to call his daughter and tell her that he was okay. They were both hesitant to call me, being worried that I might think they were crazy. Kind of funny, isn't it?

When loved ones can't seem to reach you, they'll try until eventually they find a way. I find great solace in knowing that Dad was able to send energy to soothe me through others. We should all be grateful for those kinds of signs and messages; they're priceless.

I hired mariachis for Dad's funeral, and of course I had them play "My Way." In addition, Marines came for the flag ceremony and one of them played "Taps." Dad had been so proud to have served his country. I planned the funeral he would have wanted and a wake he would have found amusing, with lots of pictures, stories, and good friends. I knew that Dad was going to be there at his funeral and wake; I wanted to give him a send-off that he could revel in. I did, and now I try to live without regret. The only thing that was strange was that I didn't clearly see him the way I usually see the "guest of honor" at a memorial service.

We do whatever we need to in order to process our pain, and I grieved in my own way. I felt that if I heard "Be strong!" one more time, I was going to scream. I didn't want to be strong, and furthermore I didn't want to worry about doing or saying the right thing. If you can't fall apart after losing your father, then when can you? Death is all about falling apart. You have to fall apart so that you can rebuild yourself. My dad died, and I am not the same person anymore. I will never be that person again, but I have learned from his death. It has definitely added several new layers to who I am as a medium.

I try to observe the strengths of those who have passed and incorporate them into myself. One of my father's strengths was laughter. He had a good time and so did everyone around him. People loved him because he made them feel good about themselves. I now make an extra effort to be social, to stop and smell the roses with my friends. The biggest compliment you can pay to people you have loved and lost is to keep a part of them alive in yourself, memorializing their significance.

Seven weeks after my dad's passing, my friend Randy died of a heart attack at age forty-nine. As I sat grieving with his three teenagers and his beautiful wife, I realized that Randy's kids were not only proud of their father, they were also aware that he'd had a terrific life. They were mourning, but every other statement was about something Randy had achieved or had taught them.

Erica, Randy's exceptional nineteen-year-old, said, "My dad will never walk me down the aisle at my wedding. He won't be there to see his grandchildren."

What could I say? She was right. How unfair was that? I realized how lucky I was to have had my dad for thirty years. Some people have even less time, or none at all.

But she wasn't waiting for my answer; she went right into another great story from one of their many summers at the lake. Looking down, Randy is surely proud of his phenomenal kids.

"My Way" was played at Randy's memorial, too. I sobbed, processing what I hadn't finished at my dad's funeral. Once again, the song was perfectly fitting.

Part of the reason I wrote this chapter is that so many people out there beat themselves up over the death of a loved one. They think that had they just taken their mom to a doctor, had they just known sooner that something was wrong, they could have prevented the passing of those they love.

I should be an example to all. I knew that Dad was going to pass and I knew the cause. Trust me, I did *everything* to prevent it but found out it was not in my hands; it never had been. When I am given information from the other side that benefits my client, or even helps to save a life, I am still only a vehicle. The information was going to get to them one way or another; I happened to be the conduit. But when someone's number is up, it's up. I hope I can help alleviate the guilt of failing to see a sign that could prevent a death. My father's story should serve as a reminder to all that sometimes it's just not in our hands.

My friend Alison sees how the deaths of our two wonderful fathers show both sides of the coin: my dad's quick and unexpected, her dad's slow and drawn out. There are gifts in both. Almost all experiences offer some gifts; they're there if you look. Sometimes they're hard to recognize through the tears, but you'll see them eventually.

Now I celebrate Dad's life. I've learned to know and love my dad even better since his passing. As I went through his belongings, searching for a shred of him, I kept rediscovering him. I found him in the many checks he'd written to Feed the Children and other kids' charities. I found him in his box of dance trophies dating back to the early 1960s. I found him in the cards I'd given him over the years and the stick-figure illustrations that I drew for him as a child. He was in the faces of my children in the photos I sorted through with a heavy heart. As I claimed his cherished belongings, I decided to reclaim him. For he is not really gone.

To my father I say, "Until we meet again, Dad! I love you, but you already know that."

My dad had a saying he concluded conversations with: "Cha cha cha, que sera, sera." He always knew that whatever will be, will be.

Chapter 2

A Little Girl Meets the Other Side

In 1978, at the ripe old age of six, I saw my first glimpse of the other side (at least, the first glimpse that I can remember). My great-grandpa Johnson died after a long battle with intestinal cancer. I remember my mom crying because Grandpa was in such excruciating pain, and he had always been so good to her. His death seemed long and drawn out.

I went to his funeral, but I didn't really understand what was going on. I remember Great-grandpa's casket being so high off the ground that I couldn't say good-bye. Mom had to pick me up so that I could look at him one last time.

Great-grandpa Johnson often wore a cowboy hat. He was a tall, friendly man who loved children. I would miss playing with him. I whispered good-bye and then I hid behind my mom, looking for an escape.

I wanted to understand what was happening. Why was everybody sobbing? I just tried to stay out of the way while my big brother Michael was busy trying to force me to touch Great-grandpa's cold hand. This petrified me. It was a long, sad day.

That night I was awakened from my sleep by a presence. My room was filled with a soft glow. I wasn't scared, but I was on edge.

Great-grandpa Johnson stood at the foot of my bed and said, "I am okay, I am still with you. Tell your mom there's no more pain."

I wanted to call for Mom, but I was paralyzed and awestruck. I wanted her to see him and know that he wasn't sick anymore. I wanted her to see that he was back, or so I thought. Great-grandpa lingered for only a moment after giving his message, and then he was gone.

What was going on? One minute he was back, and the next he was gone again. Didn't he want to stay?

I got out of bed and went down the hall to sit next to Mom's door. I knew what had happened was not typical. Mom had never talked about seeing people again after their funerals. I was worried that she might think

I was making up stories and that I'd get in trouble. But I told her anyway. The experience was too special to keep to myself. I had to share it with her; Great-grandpa said so.

My mom did what most parents would do. She smiled, said, "Of course I believe you," and then turned away.

But I knew she didn't believe me. I felt so misunderstood. Her reaction, although normal, started me on a journey of denial and confusion. My logical little mind started churning. If I had only imagined seeing my great-grandpa, then he hadn't really visited me.

I had always been told I had a vivid imagination, so I decided to keep these imaginative moments to myself. After the subject of Great-grandpa was dropped, I dismissed psychic occurrences and ignored all messages from the other side. Sometimes I thought I was hallucinating. I could see faded human figures standing next to people. Colorful personal information about strangers popped into my head and ran from beginning to end like a movie. I convinced myself that my mind was bored and was creating visions. But I was tired of visual congestion. I was overloaded by the other side and I didn't even know it.

As a psychic child, I needed to be encouraged to talk about my ability, but how could my mom have known what I needed? It is not commonly known in our society how to help young psychics develop their gifts. One of the reasons I wrote this book is to assist parents and their gifted children in avoiding misunderstanding and confusion. I want to prevent young people from turning away from their gift, and instead to embrace it early in life.

Chapter 3

Angel on My Shoulder

I was an awkward eleven-year-old. My legs looked like a foal's, long and knobby-kneed. My hair was long, curly, and red. My cheeks were covered with freckles, which I hated. But to an outsider, I looked like any other American girl without a care in the world. Like most sheltered children, I fell a little on the naive side.

One afternoon, I was riding my bicycle home from playing at a girlfriend's house in my neighborhood, concentrating on what my mom had made for dinner. As I turned the corner, I passed an alley that was lined with middle-class wooden fences. Just then, a car pulled up beside me with two young men in it.

The man on the passenger side leaned out of his window toward me. With his long hair, he looked a little like my big brother,

Michael. I thought maybe this was one of his friends. We lived in a cul-de-sac, so most of the teenagers driving this direction were there to visit him.

The moments that followed are burned into my memory forever.

He smiled and said, "You need a ride home?"

"No thank you," I replied. My mom had taught me that being polite was important. "I live right around the corner. I'm almost home."

Then he said, "Come on, it will be fun! Come drive around with us."

I looked around. There was nobody in any of the front yards, nobody driving down Thirty-second Street, nobody around at all. My stomach felt sick. Something wasn't right, but I couldn't move.

A voice sounded in my ear: *Go! Take off!* Images of my house flashed urgently in my head over and over again. The voice startled me out of my paralyzed fear and I took off on my bike for my house. The car with the two men peeled out in the opposite direction and sped down Thirty-second Street. My chest hurt from holding my breath out of fear. I rode home as fast as I could and told my mom what had happened.

She did what the majority of parents do

when confronted with this situation: She opted not to call the police. Having spent years promoting child safety, I know that, unfortunately, most attempted child abductions go unreported by the parents.

That same year a paperboy was abducted and sexually assaulted in my neighborhood. I know in my heart that if I had stayed put even thirty seconds longer, I would have been pulled through the window of that car and been a victim of a violent crime. I also know that because I listened to that powerful, authoritative voice on that hot afternoon in 1983, I am here to share my life story with my readers. I listened and I survived. Listen to your guides, whether you feel they are angels, family members on the other side, or simply guardians. They try to guide us through life safely and successfully, so pay attention to them. Don't dismiss them. Don't question whether they are really there — they are.

That same year, I remember, I saw a TV movie called *Adam*. It was the story of Adam Walsh, a six-year-old boy who had been abducted, murdered, and decapitated. As I watched the movie, I realized what abductors could do to kids. I was so sheltered that I had no idea that such awful things could happen. I realized what the two men could have done to me had I stayed any longer.

I did not understand why people hurt kids, but I knew that it was wrong. I knew that somehow other adults could help stop bad people from hurting kids. I vowed to myself that when I grew up I was going to do something to protect children from predators. It would probably be through politics or law. I wasn't big enough yet, but I would be someday.

I remember my fear of abduction turning to anger and then into a plan. Within a year I wrote a school paper discussing my future career. I was going to be a prosecuting attorney, and someday I would be the judge who dealt out harsh punishment to people who hurt children. My path was already being defined. I felt the calling to turn the tide against child predators.

Almost two decades later, in November 2000, my life's goal would reemerge as a result of a missing-person case in Texas that led me toward helping to establish a child abduction alert system in Arizona. I will be discussing that in the next chapter.

If I can provide law enforcement with perpetrator information that helps point them in the right direction, then I have helped in the fight against a lowlife. Balancing the scales is the reason I do what I do. If someone who hurts a child is held accountable, then society as a whole can rest easier. If I can help to ease the pain of a victim's family members and somehow make their hearts lighter, then the heavy nature of the tasks I undertake is well worth it.

I know now that when I pedaled my bike home on that frightening day in my twelfth year that there was an angel on my shoulder, setting me on the path that I would follow as an adult.

Chapter 4

Missing

As a college freshman, at age nineteen, I sat in my first political science class. As I listened to my professor lecturing each day, chronicling the details of various wars, I grew increasingly interested in how a political strategist could finesse a dangerous situation. It occurred to me that such people need not only historical knowledge to draw on but also an apparent instinct for defusing potential crises. Political strategists have played important roles in behind-the-scenes American security.

Now I was torn between wanting to be a lawyer and wanting to be a political strategist. I had a knack for knowing what people were going to do before they did it, and I often received a mental picture of a criminal while watching news reports of unsolved cases. But I was still too young and inexperienced to realize the extent of my ability. I was unwilling to think of myself as different from others. It would take more time and a chain of complicated events to bring that awareness and acceptance.

As of today, I have worked on numerous missing person cases. I profile for law enforcement and I assist the friends and families of murdered people. I can access both the victims' and the perpetrators' minds. I find I'm more effective if I access the perpetrators, because they tend to run more on adrenaline, meaning that they are processing it in their minds, rather than their hearts or their souls. Tapping into what someone is thinking is easier for me than sensing what someone is feeling. I aim for the most information in the shortest amount of time, so less emotion helps to bring through more coherent information. Unfortunately, most abduction cases do not have the happy ending we'd all like them to have.

Most people don't realize that there are plenty of competent psychic profilers (although the psychic part isn't always acknowledged) out there who assist law enforcement every day. Understand that often we cannot take any credit for our work because it can legally hinder a case. The defense would have a field day in court with psychic intervention, and we don't want to discredit the prosecution or do anything to weaken a case.

Law enforcement is also hesitant to acknowledge our role because of the controversy surrounding psychics. Having family in law enforcement, and having worked in the field myself, I can understand why this is the case.

Psychics are physically and emotionally drained by work on missing persons' cases. It takes a great deal of energy to access both perpetrators and victims. It opens us up to things most people never experience. For these reasons, some psychics choose not to work missing persons' cases.

Aside from being draining, the job is often thankless. Those who choose to do it want to make a difference. I was given the ability to see into criminal minds, and I won't squander that gift. At the same time, I work on only a limited number of cases per year so that I don't burn out. (For the record, I've never asked for or accepted payment for my work on any such case.)

If I cannot provide specific, helpful details I will not work a case. I prefer not to work personally with a family but rather to work with police, friends of the family, and so on. I profile to help people, not hurt them.

While working as a child advocate in a

nonpsychic context, I was able to talk with some parents of missing children who had previously used psychics for help. I was dumbfounded at what they had been told by these callous opportunists. They had been given hurtful, traumatic details of their children's abductions, but they had been led no closer to finding the children or the perpetrators. The psychics then charged money for inflicting such pain upon them.

I cannot tell you how upsetting this is to me. It makes me hot with anger for these parents and their children, because I spend my life trying to lend credibility to my gift.

I hope that by providing some guidelines for young psychics and mediums, I can help prevent them from becoming the types who injure their clients and damage our field. Nothing is more difficult than a loved one's death, especially a child's. If such details as "She was in excruciating pain" or "She screamed for her mother" are pertinent to a case (which is unlikely), offer them to the police, not to the family. Those who add salt to an already painful wound are not only unethical, they are without mercy or conscience.

In August 2000, I had an opportunity to work with Texas law enforcement on my first official missing person case. This case will always be special to me, and it resulted in something that I will forever be proud of.

I had provided law enforcement with specific details about the perpetrator in the abduction and murder of a little girl; this information had not been released to the public. They were so taken aback by the information that they wanted to meet with me personally.

I was planning a trip to Virginia to do a media interview and made arrangements to catch a connecting flight in Dallas, where I was met at the airport by a group of noble-looking Rangers. They were tall, polite, and ready to go. One of my favorites was the sergeant. He was very Texan, and I mean that as a compliment. I was as amused by him as he was by me.

During our car ride, he turned to me and said, "Tell me something about myself." He said it in a friendly way, so I didn't mind.

"Oh, a test! Like I don't deal with that every day of my life." I paused, smiled, and said, "You have a serious problem with your heart; you need to pay special attention to your health."

He and the spirited female police officer riding with us burst out laughing.

"What's so funny?"

"I just had double bypass surgery on my heart," the sergeant said.

I told him not to cheat on his prescribed health routine. (Unfortunately, he called me a few months later to tell me that he'd had another heart attack.)

We spent a few hours driving and covered the many areas where the perpetrator claimed to have taken the little girl. The perpetrator was a compulsive liar, so I eliminated the false areas for the police. (Many serial killers like to keep the location of their victims secret; they know that it gives them power over law enforcement and society.) Incidentally, the police had already eliminated some of the areas; they just thought they'd test me. I traipsed around in the wooded areas and stepped over animal carcasses, animal skeletons, and so on. I wish I'd had my gun with me; it was straight out of a horror flick. The Rangers had a clear advantage, and they promised they wouldn't let the tarantulas get me.

I saw the barbed-wire fence I had described, and the area where I was walking was near a major marker that I'd pointed out on a map before coming to Texas. The information I had given them earlier agreed with that provided by the killer's accomplices, and I learned that I had correctly described the vehicle used in the child's abduction; also I had stated correctly that the perpetrator had switched vehicles during the abduction. It's always a little creepy to see your visions unfold.

Night fell and we were unable to cover the rest of the area. I had a morning flight and had to leave without continuing the search. My hiking boots and I would have to come back another time. I was frustrated. I had been looking for evidence of the child's death and it seemed my efforts had been in vain. In an odd coincidence, tropical storm Allison came in and flooded the area shortly thereafter.

The Rangers and other law enforcement officers I'd worked with were brave, honorable people with tears in their eyes over this child. I left disappointed, and I asked my guides, "Why? Why did you send me there if I wasn't supposed to find her?"

The answer to that question would come in three months. When I returned to Phoenix, I recalled that the Texas police sergeant had told me about a system called the

Amber Alert, named after Amber Hager-man, who was abducted and murdered in 1996. It's a child abduction alert system that is used to inform the public as soon as the police have determined that an abduction has occurred. Local radio and TV stations interrupt their broadcasting with a description of the suspect, vehicle, and child, giving drivers and residents a chance to save a child by notifying the police of his or her whereabouts.

I decided to write to local politicians to see if I could initiate the establishment of an Amber Alert system in Phoenix. I contacted local missing persons organizations asking for their help, but to no avail. So I did the work on my own. Of the many letters I wrote, I received a response from only one politician, but one politician was all I needed. I was asked to serve on the task force to design the alert and I was honored to do so.

I chose to remain anonymous until the alert system was made public and put into use because I didn't want to diminish its credibility in any way. (It made me sad, but I was just being realistic.) Meanwhile, a year passed and the alert system still hadn't been introduced to the public. I was beginning to grow impatient. In March, three years to the very day since the little girl in Texas had been abducted, the alert system was spontaneously unveiled in Maricopa County. The Texas girl was not only the reason for my learning about the alert, but also, I believe, the reason that I had so much help moving it along.

A whole chain of events had to occur in order for me to bring my hometown alert alive. Now children in Arizona will have a chance to survive what the little girl in Texas didn't. I think it's no coincidence that the alert system was unveiled in Phoenix on the anniversary of her abduction. It is true that everything happens for a reason.

Two months after being unveiled, the alert brought back a little girl who had been taken by her non-custodial dad. He had made some questionable statements that could be interpreted as physical threats. A trucker spotted her dad's license plate and she was recovered three hours later.

I was asked by a local news station whether it was a mistake to activate the alert in a parental abduction. My response was that parental abduction should not be exempted if a child may be in danger. It's a call that the police have to make on a case-by-case basis, and I think they made the right one. The abducted girl was home safe and sound with her mother for Thanksgiving dinner that week.

The Maricopa County alert went on to save a baby who was in the backseat during a carjacking just two months later. Countless children have been saved thanks to this clever alert system.

The little Texas girl's remains were recovered in January 2004, and she was finally brought home to her family. I was able both to confirm the correct information that I had provided to the police and to learn from the markers (physical clues and locations) that I misread.

For example, I kept seeing small airplanes (not commercial) and later I kicked myself for not being more vigilant: I should have narrowed the location of remains to areas near airports, Air Force bases, and so on. The body was located a mile from an Air Force base. I had said over and over she was by government land, large parks and barbed wire fences. I kept seeing the word "pueblo," and as it turned out, Pueblo Trail was near the area of her remains. I also kept seeing "Timber," and Timber Wolf Lane was near the area.

This type of search is not an exact science, and not all information may be confirmed. But many of the markers I receive can be helpful when properly applied. I could have narrowed the search to a square mile. That may sound like a huge area, but when police are looking for a small child in the state of Texas, narrowing the search to a mile is excellent. Sometimes it's not in the grand plan that profilers ever find the murder victim. Sometimes others' lives are supposed to be affected by the discovery of a body — for instance, a hiker may be meant to stumble upon someone's remains.

Remember, real life is the only way for head-tappers to learn and become effective. In the four years since I worked on this case I've sharpened my skills considerably, but I will never forget that little girl in Texas who forever changed my life through her whispers.

✦ *Elizabeth Smart*

Everyone I came across in 2002 wanted to know what I thought about Elizabeth Smart's abduction. Since the outcome of her case was not only happy but miraculous, I will share some of the pertinent details. Before her return, I had shared this information with a reputable search-and-rescue team that was deployed to Utah.

In June 2002, Elizabeth Smart was abducted from her home. Her heartbreaking story was on every major news program in America. The nation watched as the Smart family searched desperately for their daughter. We were all witness to every parent's worst nightmare.

I, like everybody else, saw Elizabeth's picture on TV and wished I could help. But I don't make a practice of giving information on a case unless I am asked for my input. Soon after the abduction, my friend Catherine asked me to provide a profile of the perpetrator to be sent to the search-and-rescue team in Utah. All the information I provided is on record and verifiable.

In my profile I stated that the perpetrator had the name Brian connected to him. I stated that he had worked for the Smarts as a groundskeeper/handyman. He was a transient, but he managed to function in society. He would often change his appearance, and I was picking up on a strong connection to California, so he might have fled there or been from there. He had pedophilic tendencies, with a possible history of acting on them. I also described a small town outside the city where Elizabeth was abducted as being a place that he'd reside or spend a lot of time. It was somehow significant to him.

I also knew that he'd taken Elizabeth to a forest area, a setting with pine trees.

As the authorities later learned, the man arrested in the kidnapping of Elizabeth Smart was Brian David Mitchell. He had worked for the Smarts briefly as a groundskeeper/handyman. He was a drifter who just a decade prior had been a family man. When he abducted Elizabeth, he held her in a forestlike campground area; he later took her to San Diego, California. His ex-wife alleged that Brian was a pedophile.

Unfortunately, none of my information was acted on when I first shared it. It was only discovered to be accurate after Elizabeth was recognized on the street by an observant stranger, who notified the authorities.

These details could have helped much sooner if they had been used. If my information couldn't help identify the perpetrator and thus help lead us to the victim, I wouldn't even bother to profile. The name of the perpetrator and his association to the victim are key, but the information is only useful if it is put to use. I hope someday the system will recognize people like me who are legitimate so that our insights can be shared with the proper authorities as soon as a kidnapping occurs. Otherwise, what good is this gift?

Once again, ours isn't a perfect science. Profilers are still human beings who will have margins of error, like everyone else. But there is no doubt that profiling can help victims. It is an ability that must be acknowledged, because the stakes are so high: human life.

✦ Lost in the Desert

One day I received a call from my mentor, Catherine, who is also a medium; she and I have held many group sessions as a duo. One of the ladies from a group session had a sister whose friends were missing. I had been watching the situation unfold on the news for a couple of days and it was receiving a lot of local coverage.

The general assumption was that the three missing people might have been carjacked and possibly killed. Steve Cerqua, his wife, Kathy, and Kathy's mother had all disappeared. There were records of ATM withdrawals and a record of the family shopping at a local store, but they hadn't been heard from since. I accepted Catherine's request for me to help them, and received a phone call from some of the missing people's relatives on the second day after their disappearance.

I started by asking who drove the Toyota Camry. I knew the Cerquas and Sally Rosenwinkel weren't driving one when they disappeared, because I'd seen a description of their vehicle on the news, but I needed to confirm that I'd made the right connection. I was told that the Cerquas' daughter drove a Camry that she often parked in their driveway.

Good! I had the right person. I was connecting with Steve Cerqua. I told the family that all three were alive and not to worry. I added that the missing trio would be found within five days of their disappearance and that they would return safely.

The family wanted to know why Steve hadn't used his cell phone to call them.

"He couldn't use it where he was. It wouldn't work," I told them.

They wanted to know the obvious: Why were their relatives missing?

I told them that the vehicle the couple was driving was not capable of going where Steve had wanted it to go. It was stuck in mud or something thick. Also, Steve had felt pretty comfortable with his navigating ability, and that had something to do with his making a driving error.

Their daughter wanted to know if her dad

would leave her mother and grandmother to go for help, and I said yes. The friends and family of the missing group had mixed feelings about that. They found it hard to believe that he'd ever leave his wife. I told them that he had no other choice; he would do it to save them. Then I gave the general location of the missing trio, saying that they were farther away than people thought, and I described a lake and picnic area nearby.

The missing couple's daughter was able to retain some hope that indeed her parents were alive. Catherine insisted that I call the detective on the case and give him my input, which I did. Unfortunately, the police didn't seem to think my information was valid, and they did not want my help.

The three dehydrated people were rescued four days after their disappearance. Steve had been trying to take a shortcut and his 4X2 got stuck in the mud. He couldn't use his cell phone because of the mountains. Finally, on the fourth day, he left Kathy and his mother-in-law to attempt to climb a nearby mountain from the top of which he hoped to obtain phone reception. He was gone for hours, but was successful in placing a call for help. A local news helicopter arrived to assist them.

Steve and Kathy celebrated their twenty-fifth wedding anniversary later that week in Hawaii. When they returned, they had a party for all of those who helped out during their disappearance. I was not able to attend, but Catherine did, and she said it was a wonderful evening. The family made a scrapbook with all of the news clippings from their disappearance, including a page designated for the psychics who worked on their case. It just doesn't get any better than that!

The Cerqua story will always remind me that missing persons can actually be alive and well. I live for cases like theirs! Even though my information didn't actually save them, it provided great comfort to their loved ones during their absence. I refer to this story whenever I need to remember a happy ending.

✦ Head Tapping

Profiling is not just about dealing with mysteries and criminals. Sometimes it involves probing the minds of people who are involved in situations that are not matters of life and death. I was once useful in helping a client locate millions of dollars in inheritance money. I did this through a phone reading, without being given any information: I brought through the sitter's deceased father, who said his daughter had inheritance money coming and told me where it was. I provided her with the country where the money could be found and told her whom she should contact for proof of its existence. She located the money and the person who had the proof.

I also receive many calls from people trying to get information about loved ones who are up to something. There's nothing like tapping into a person's head and then having to tell my client that I see his wife near a bar in a parking lot meeting another man. I almost always receive word back. Without fail, my client calls back to confirm my information and then adds that this isn't the first time the spouse had strayed.

Sometimes a husband will think his wife has been abducted when in fact she has run off. It's a little distracting to get a distress call, only to find that she is not a victim, that the husband knew that it was a possibility that she was out carousing. I prefer to be left out of these situations.

If I tap into a person's head when he or she is drunk or on drugs, I can feel the dulling, slowing effects myself. I also feel their emotions. Head tapping is interesting, because it allows me to really get into some-one's thoughts. However, children who have been brutally traumatized are usually inac-cessible to me. I have to get my information from the perpetrator's head, not the child's. The child was usually too confused to know what was really happening, so it's more dif-ficult to read.

I am also used for jury selection in rape/homicide cases, in order to obtain the sen-tence the prosecution wants. I only work with prosecution teams I am familiar with. Also, I only work cases where there is no doubt the defendant committed the crime. I want the information I receive to be backed up by DNA evidence. I do not take what I do lightly.

I have been asked if that's stacking the deck against the defense. First of all, I hope so. Second, I am only choosing from a pool of potential jurors already selected by our justice system. Finally, I have to say that de-fense attorneys would try to discredit people like me anyway. If I can't do what I say I can do, if they are right in saying that my information is unreliable, then they have nothing to worry about. Besides, the prose-cutors ultimately go with their own final de-cisions.

One case that I took more personally than most was the death of a witness who was going to be testifying in court the next day. She was also a mother, and her children were in the house when she was murdered in cold blood.

Being a mother, I gave this one everything I had to give; it consumed me. The defendant had no remorse. What most people didn't see was that the victim herself was there in the courtroom every day of that trial. On the day of closing arguments, I walked into the courtroom while fumbling through my oversized purse in search of my lipstick. Just then, I heard a soft female voice say, "That's my boy!"

I glanced to my left and the murder victim was sitting beside me, smiling. I looked up and saw the back of a young man's head. Just then the prosecutor walked up with a young man he introduced as the victim's son Neil, and we shook hands.

This was another one of the defendant's casualties, one who would become a strong and significant man in spite of the thug who killed his mother. In my thoughts I heard, "You're here for him. You fight for him!"

I gave Neil a ride home that day. He

opened his wallet to show me his mom's picture, one of many family pictures in his wallet. That said it all.

I gave him my phone number and told him to call me if he ever needed anything at all. He said thanks and we parted ways. He never knew the extent of what I do. It wasn't necessary. All he needed to know was that I was a jury consultant who cared about his mom's case.

Meanwhile, the lead prosecutor was growing very concerned about jurors having to be excused and replaced at the last minute. On Saturday I attended a party at the prosecutor's house. She was frazzled, wanting to know when the jury would come back with the sentence and what that sentence would be.

"Boy, they don't ask for much, do they?" I thought sarcastically. I shot back at her: "Tuesday at three the jury will come back in favor of the prosecution's plea for the death penalty."

She smiled and said she felt a little better, but she still had that huge knot in her stomach. After all, a lot was riding on her ability.

The case had begun to take a toll on my health, and I caught a cold over the weekend. I found comfort in getting sauced on cold medicine. Tuesday morning rolled around and my weary eyes opened to look at the clock. It was 9:30; the jury had just gone into deliberation. I was sick to my stomach, but it wasn't from my cold. I felt the weight of the prosecution on my shoulders, as well as that of the victim and her children. I wanted to bring them some justice and let those kids know that their mom mattered.

I also wanted to make sure that this murderer was never released to kill again, and there was plenty of evidence that he would have done just that. My head felt as if it was in a vise all morning. Eventually it was three o'clock. I picked up the phone to call the prosecutor, hoping that she had gotten a verdict.

She picked up the line immediately. "We just got the call! The jury is back with their sentence! I've got to go; I'll call you when it's over. And Allison, just so you know — the jury came back at two fifty-seven p.m."

We hung up as I watched the clock ticking. I drove to the mall to do an errand, my heart pounding and a lump in my throat the entire time.

After half an hour the phone rang. I almost jumped out of my skin.

"Hello?"

"Allison, you're good."

"Did we get the death penalty?"

"Yes."

I had to know: "What did the defendant do when it was read?"

"He laughed."

A happy ending. But I want to emphasize that I alone didn't achieve these results. It took a lot of good police work and the right, gifted legal team to make this happen. It also took the bravery of the young children who will always remain a part of their mother.

After every case I say to myself, "This is my life." Some people say they could never do my job even if they had the ability to. I can understand. It's a tall order, but for some reason I can't do anything else.

Chapter 5

Kindergarten Mediums

My six-year-old daughter, Ariel, came home from school one day upset because her peers weren't able to see the apparition of a man who stood in the hall in front of her classroom at school. She described him to them and her classmates laughed at her. When she turned around, he was gone.

I found out later that Ariel's friend Erin had leaned over and whispered, "I can see him too, Ariel." I am so tickled that Ariel has a friend her age with the same gift, so she doesn't feel so alienated. Ariel and Erin talk to each other about their abilities and about what I do. They know that not everyone can see the things they do, and that that's okay. They like having their special powers.

I want to share some exercises I use with my girls to help prevent them from shutting down as they get older. I've noticed that once little psychics realize their peers think they're weird or different, they tend to ignore or block their ability to communicate with the other side. The last thing school-age children want is to stand out and be teased by others.

When my girls are grown, they can decide for themselves whether they want to maintain a relationship with the other side. Until then, I will try to keep my kids open to the possibilities that surround them.

When I shut down as a child, it was because of confusion about what I was seeing and hearing, as well as my mom's ambivalence, that made me afraid to disappoint her. I hope that this chapter might help parents find out whether a child has a psychic gift, as well as suggest what to do once they are certain that the child does.

Say your child comes to you and says, "Mommy, I see a woman over there." You look over and see nothing. What should you do? You should turn to your child and say, "Really? What does she look like? What is her name? Does she want to tell us something?"

Plenty of children have imaginary friends and love to make up stories. If that's the case with your child, you have done no harm in listening to his or her story and playing along. And if something more significant is going on, you are doing your best to reassure your child that it's okay.

You might find that a friend or relative on the other side is hanging around your child and trying to communicate with you through him. This is a great exercise for enabling your child to become comfortable telling you details of his spiritual encounters. It also encourages your child to think about asking questions and exploring the possibility of communicating with something others may not see. You will remove the strangeness surrounding it, which is important. The first person a child looks to for comfort, approval, and learning is his parents. You set the tone for your child's development of his gift.

Children are easier for spirits to access than adults are. Adults have issues and emotional walls built up that can make it difficult for a spirit to come through to them. Often a spirit has whispered messages or tried to be seen by a loved one, only to be dismissed.

Knowing that my children are being watched over gives me a feeling of warmth and added security. Some people might say, "I wasn't close to Aunt Emma, so why is she with me?" The person on the other side may have died around the time you were born, or maybe she felt connected to one of your parents and now chooses to be with you. That's all that matters. We have to realize as human beings that sometimes something bigger than us can call the shots. Feel loved and connected and try not to get bogged down in the whys, because eventually we all receive the answers to our questions.

✦ Testing 1–2–3

As an exercise for my oldest daughter, I challenge her to find missing objects around the house.

My husband, Joe, was missing his electric shaver for a few days and had to use a disposable. Let's just say I was worried about becoming a widow. I was sure that Joe was going to bleed to death after using a regular razor. We figured that our one-year-old, Marie, had toddled off with the electric shaver and left it missing in action.

I was in bed with the flu, so I called Ariel over and told her I had something to ask of her. I'll admit that at first I was a typical mom and tried bribing her for two days with monetary gain if she would tell me where the razor was. Anyone who knows

Ariel also knows that shopping is her favorite thing to do; she has a clear appreciation of money. Still, no luck; she said she didn't know where the razor was.

After a few days, I took a different approach. One morning as Ariel stood next to my bed, I said to her, "Close your eyes and take a deep cleansing breath, and exhale so that I can hear you. Is your mind a blank canvas? Are you relaxed? Now, where is Dad's electric shaver? What is the first thing that comes to your mind?"

"It's in a drawer, I think, in Marie's room."

I went to Marie's room and looked in her dresser; it wasn't there, but since Ariel was seeing the razor in a drawer, I stepped three feet away from the dresser to the door of Marie's room, and there reached for the first drawer in the hall. Bingo! Joe's electric razor. I told Ariel that although it wasn't actually in Marie's room, it was very close and that was good work, especially considering the size of our two-story house.

Being close but not exact is a common experience. Sometimes a psychic or medium has a hit, just not a direct hit. Taking into consideration Ariel's age and lack of experience, her information was impressive, and I let her know it. By positively supporting Ariel, I piqued her interest in psychic games, which is critical in preventing a child from closing her mind to her gift.

Encourage your kids to trust their first instincts and the original information received. They shouldn't alter the information by mixing in preconceived notions. This was a great exercise; Ariel saw it as a challenging game and enjoyed it. At the same time it has strengthened her psychic capabilities, and the ability to locate objects is one of the most useful of all psychic tools. Ariel is learning to trust what she gets and to be comfortable enough with her gift to share it with me.

I tell my daughter not to shout from the rooftops about her gift, because not all people understand what they can't see. I also tell her to appreciate and honor her talents because they are special. Encourage your kids, but don't force it on them. If they are uncomfortable doing these exercises, then back off.

If your child approaches you, be open to talking freely about anything. This subject should only be approached if your child seems confused by a related matter or directly comes to you with premonitions or questions about the other side. We don't want to confuse kids who don't really have psychic abilities.

If you see such strong signs in your child that you can't ignore them, try sharing a story about a family member who has the gift (I believe the sixth sense is most often genetic). Talk to your child about angels or about Grandpa in heaven. The child will be more comfortable opening up if you are personally extending yourself.

Don't beat your child over the head with a two-hour discussion, especially if it seems to be a one-way talk. Slide the topic out there, see if your child reciprocates, and take it slowly. If your child is uninterested, drop it. When and if your child wants to talk, the discussion can resume.

If your child's gift is causing fear, it's important to address that carefully. I tell my guides to monitor the energy that comes around my kids and to keep out any negative or mischievous energy. Let your child know that she has the power to tell the energy to leave, if it's not welcome. This technique is effective for anyone, big or small. It's important for kids to know that spirits cannot harm them.

My oldest daughter occasionally comes to me and says that she feels crowded. By this I know she means that she is experiencing strong spirit activity and is feeling the people she sometimes can't see. Fortunately, what Ariel can't see I can, because I have more experience and know how to retrieve a visual of the spirit at will.

I tell her to ask the presence some basic questions, such as "Who are you?" and "What do you want?" If her discomfort continues after she receives an answer, I tell the spirit that it's frightening her and must go. I also tell my daughter that if she's frightened she should envision herself draped in a beautiful powerful cloak of white light. She loves clothes, so I've incorporated her personality into this exercise so that it's comforting and familiar to her. I tell her that the cloak of light will protect her from things that frighten her.

Ariel refers to her guides as her "angels" (the term she's comfortable with). They watch over her and make her feel safe, which in turn makes me happy. A child's security and feeling of comfort and safety are always a priority.

Another reason for my daughter's discomfort would be that she is absorbing too much energy all at once. By this I mean that sensitive people (those who are extremely empathetic or feel other people's energy around them) sometimes feel bombarded by too many energies at once. This type of thing can happen to anyone. Most people have had the experience of standing next to someone and for no apparent reason being repelled, not by the person's appearance, but by a feeling that they get from him or her.

Just as often, people are drawn to others who seem to have an approachable energy or an energy similar to theirs. People have their own individual energies and, like personalities, these energies vary. What one person finds attractive, another person might find repellent. The more people are clustered around you, the more variations of energy you take in.

If you're sensitive by nature, everything in life feels magnified. Picture one person who is arrogant and self-centered getting right in your face. Then add an annoying person who is giggly and mischievous; next, add a loud, heavy talker. Are you feeling uncomfortable yet? This can be what contact with others' energy feels like for a medium.

If you have heightened senses, other human beings don't even have to be in your face to feel as if they are. You must therefore establish boundaries for yourself and try to keep yourself in an atmosphere you find comfortable. Some people don't mind having their personal space invaded. I find that these are usually the very same people who tend to invade the space of others.

Personally, I try to avoid crowded situations like concerts or busy shopping days. Too much sensory overload. I like smaller, quieter venues. My husband is an aerospace engineer. I find Joe's company gatherings pleasant enough, because engineering generally draws pretty laid-back people. This I can handle. On the other hand, a high school football game is too much for me. Don't get me wrong, I love young people. I am just too sensitive for a stadium full of electric, hormonal teenage energy.

When Ariel overloaded once at an amusement park, I found a quiet corner and sat down with her to calm her. We talked about how she was feeling and shared some valuable mother-daughter time. I really understood how she felt. Since we had been at the amusement park for a while, I suggested we go back to our hotel and unwind.

Ariel insisted that before we leave we visit a century-old house located in the park. She seemed excited about it, so I agreed. Ariel went to one side of the house and I went to the other. Ariel came tearing around the corner, smiling.

"Mom! Come over on this side of the house! It has the most activity!"

Ariel and I share a love of old houses. We

enjoy seeing the spirits who inhabit buildings and sampling the time period from which they lived. To my family this is normal living; there's never a dull moment. I am proud and honored to share in my children's gifts and ease them through their journeys.

If you are trying to determine whether your child is a medium or has had contact with the other side, take note of some of the signs I looked for with my own kids. I know firsthand what terms I am likely to hear from another person with this gift, as well as what questions to expect from inexperienced or young mediums. After all, I've been there.

The criteria I use to determine a child's abilities are as follows:

1. Does your child ever say a room feels crowded even when it's not physically congested, or does your child seem easily flustered in certain surroundings?

Sensitive children may feel the presence of energy around them but may not be able to see any of it. Sometimes sight isn't available to the medium, which can be confusing if they are hearing, feeling, or even smelling or tasting signs from the other side. This is especially common among young mediums whose skills aren't well developed.

2. Does your child want to avoid being around a lot of people because the experience is overwhelming?

Just like adults, sensitive children absorb energy from all the people around them, and too much of it can overwhelm their systems.

3. Does your child tell you that he or she notices apparitions? Does he or she talk about "seeing things?"

If your child is able to give you personal details about a family member or close friend of yours who passed away before your child was born, that's a compelling sign that she sees the other side. Of course, be sure to ask yourself whether this information is something you talk about around the child that could be simply overheard and repeated. You want to be certain that your child is sharing information he or she couldn't possibly have learned any other way.

For example, when Ariel was two and a half she woke up in the middle of the night calling out to Joe and me. We went to her and asked what was wrong.

Ariel said, "A man was here and he said he is a jeeeneeeus."

Joe perked up. "Did you say 'genius'?"

I asked him who he thought had visited

Ariel. Joe replied that his father had always referred to himself as a genius. Since Joe's father had died three months before I met him, I knew very little of him. He was highly intellectual, with a chemical engineering degree from MIT, but his personal traits were more of a mystery to me. Ariel couldn't have known what her granddad called himself. Joe was touched and amused by the message.

The unique nature of the message told me that Ariel really had heard from her granddad, so we talked to her about what had happened. Don't dismiss your child's encounters. Young people are uninhibited; they are without walls, and thus are easier for the other side to access.

4. Is your child able to describe what he or she sees in great detail? She should be able to cite physical characteristics, objects that may have been important to the individual, possibly even a name. The information should seem clear to the child without the need to ponder it too long. For instance, my six-year-old daughter told me that my great-grandmother had a bathroom she loved, with pink tile and roses. I had to call my grandma Jenee to ask about this, because Grandma Ruth had died when I was thirteen. She confirmed that my daughter

had accurately described the bathroom in the house that they had lived in over fifty years ago.

I was a part of my youngest daughter's first reading. My dad had died about eight months earlier, and she had just turned four. One day she jumped up on my bed with a picture she had drawn of two people.

"Marie, who did you draw a picture of?"

"It's you, Mommy! And Grandpa Mike! You're dancing together."

I wasn't prepared for that.

"Honey, Grandpa died."

"No he didn't, Mommy. He's still here; he tells me so."

I realized that — much like me when I was six years old looking at Great-grandpa Johnson — she thought Grandpa Mike was still alive. Of course, in a sense they are, but children know no difference between being alive in spirit and being alive on earth.

Later, out of the blue, Marie started saying, "Cha cha cha, Mom!"

That shocked me.

"Marie, why are you saying that?"

She started dancing around the room, repeating herself.

"Grandpa Mike, that's why!"

Of course. Silly me. What was I thinking? My dad always said that. I feel so lucky to have three little reminders of my dad. Even if your kids aren't mediums, you can see those who came before them in the faces and personalities of your children.

Another example: The week after the first anniversary of my father's death, I was feeling pretty down. I didn't want to impose my heartache upon my kids, but I had several quiet moments of daydreaming about him. I thought I was pretty good at keeping them to myself. I was sitting at the kitchen table when Bridgett, my second daughter, sneaked up behind me. She leaned toward my ear to tell me a secret:

"Mom, Grandpa Mike says he doesn't like it when you're sad, and he says for me to tell you that he loves you."

Well, you could have knocked me over with a feather. I hadn't said a word about my dad. This was so meaningful to me. I get a taste of my own medicine every time one of my girls demonstrates her ability to see the unseen.

5. Does your child describe events that later come to pass? Can he or she sense where something is without traditional clues? The ability to predict events and identify locations is a strong sign of talent. Marie does this frequently. It's a hard sign to miss, and it's exciting.

Ariel does it, too. One afternoon Joe and I were preparing to drive to Tucson, which is about two hours away and a place my children have never been. We would be meeting some friends there for dinner. Before we left, Ariel said, "Mommy, look at the picture I drew."

With a marker on a white erasable board she had drawn a huge picture of an exotic-looking flower with long, very thin petals. She referred to it as the Italian flower. Joe and I praised her work and then left for our drive. We met our dinner companions at the host's house and then headed for dinner at an Italian restaurant. We walked in, and on the wall hung a huge picture of an exotic flower with long, very thin petals. Joe and I looked at each other in amazement. The picture was identical to the one that Ariel had drawn. That she had called the flower Italian made the occurrence even more significant. Even the length of the stem was the same. It was eerie, but I like that.

I'll use my four-year-old, Bridgett, as an example for parents with really young psychics. This is not a prediction, just an example of knowing something is there without using your eyes to see. This ties into locating objects psychically.

Bridgett is good at seeing what is hidden.

On a trip, our family was in a restaurant, waiting at the counter for our take-out so that we could go back to our hotel room and have a snack. The counter was about a foot higher than the top of Bridgett's head. Bridgett extended her arm straight up into the air and said, "Mommy, Mommy, can I have a piece of candy?"

Before I could ask her how she knew there was candy on top of the counter, three friendly but perplexed women standing behind us asked her that very question. Without answering, Bridgett looked around, grabbed a box from the side of the counter, pushed it up against the front of the counter, and stood on it. She peered over the edge of the counter, saw the dish of candy, then stepped down and said, "Well, there is a dish of candy up there. See?"

I had taken a good look at the front of the counter. It was solid; there was no glass to peek through. As we left, I asked her how she had known there was candy on the counter without seeing it with her eyes. Bridgett said, "I don't know, I just know these things."

A month before the candy dish episode, my mom came over to our house to watch the girls for us while we went to the toy store to buy a gift for a birthday party.

While Joe and I were at the toy store, I did something that I never do: I purchased a lollipop to put on top of the gift. When we pulled into our driveway, Bridgett came running up to the car as I opened my door to step out.

"Mommy, give me the lollipop!"

"I didn't get you a lollipop," I said.

"Well, I know you have one in the car." She was right, but how did she know? My husband was still in the car, and no one else knew.

"How did you know I had a lollipop in the car?"

Bridgett was not amused; she just wanted the lollipop. "I don't know, I just knew."

This kid is a candy, food, and beverage detector; you can't hide anything from her. There are too many other instances to share each one, but you get the idea.

✦ A Learning Problem . . . or a Gift?

Because I get so much e-mail concerning children who have behavior problems or ADD (attention deficit disorder), I felt I must address this. I have seen instances where parents have misread their child's symptoms and come to the wrong conclusions. This is an area of great controversy, and sometimes there are no easy answers.

Children with ADD are easily distracted and overstimulated. They have trouble focusing on what they are doing, so their grades often suffer. Their brains are in overdrive. However, this does not mean that the images in their minds are coming from the other side. There is no real correlation between psychic powers and other common problems such as ADD or depression. However, in my opinion, children with such problems are also no less likely to have the gift than other children. It's important for parents not to rule anything out or jump to any conclusions.

In one case, a child often spoke of suicides, so his family thought that deceased people were coming through to him. But judging by what the family said, I didn't think the boy appeared mediumistic. Something made me ask the professions of his parents. It turned out that his mother was a police dispatcher.

When parents work in this sort of field, they have to look even more closely at the child's claims. If a child's information is something he could have overheard at home, then look further. Children who are truly mediums should not be limited to sensing grim, morbid deaths. They should also be able to contact deceased friends or relatives, those with positive energy. Of course, this doesn't exclude the possibility of an encounter with dark circumstances, but they shouldn't be all a child sees.

A child may be dealing with something other than psychic phenomena, such as a chemical imbalance, depression, anxiety, or simply the need for attention. I highly recommend having the child evaluated by a physician to rule out or treat any of these possibilities. Take everything into consideration.

Chapter 6

Hormones and Teen Psychics

My mother divorced my stepdad when I was twelve, and that turned my world upside down. It is typical for a twelve-year-old to feel unstable; a divorce in the family will only add to a child's sense of insecurity. However, psychic teenagers may find adolescence even more difficult than others do.

Teens are already at the mercy of their hormones. Their emotions are riding high, and everything is a big deal. Throw in a heightened sense of awareness and the ability to literally hear what people are thinking of you, and you have a recipe for misery.

Quite honestly, during my own teen years I drank alcohol to keep myself on a more even keel. I am certainly not suggesting alcohol as an escape; it was a bad choice. Having an understanding parent and communication with other psychics would have been much more helpful. I had no support and it would have made all the difference in my youth.

For me, alcohol would temporarily soften the voices from the other side. If I had a beer in my hand, nobody thought twice when I laughed to myself in solitary conversation. Of course, it wasn't really a one-way conversation, because I was never truly alone.

Fortunately for me, I was listening on the night my guides came through with what seemed at the time to be nothing more than a decorating tip.

I was seventeen and living at my friend Susie's house. I'd known her since I was two and she was four; we grew up on the same cul-de-sac. We were best friends and partners in crime. When we were little we'd spent half a day coloring our neighborhood sidewalks to make the world a more beautiful place. After our mothers discovered our urban gallery, we spent the second half of that day scrubbing the sidewalks with soap and water. Susie and I couldn't understand how our mothers could have missed the beauty of our work.

Susie's mom, Shari, has always been like a second mom to me. She knew what my life had been like at home. I felt comfort when she took me in at such a confusing time in my young life.

I was in my room, getting ready to go out, when I heard a voice telling me to move my bed, which stood against the south wall, under my bedroom window. Without much thought, I pushed it against the east wall. Let it be known that I am not a big furniture arranger. I usually decide how I like something and then leave it alone. I stood for a moment pondering what I had just done, then quickly got over it.

Hours after I moved my bed, I embarked upon a typical weekend night. My friend Barb and I decided to go to a high school party. We finally made it back to my house at around 1:00 in the morning. Barb and I were tired from our long evening, so we went to my room and passed out (literally).

In the middle of the night I was jolted out of my sleep by a loud crash. Blinding headlights, broken cement blocks, and the front end of a truck were in my bedroom! Cement blocks had landed right on my bed and my room was filled with dust from smashed cement. I shook Barb and told her to wake up. She was in such a deep sleep the noise hadn't fazed her.

I climbed out of bed and realized that

there was a woman in the truck; her face was bleeding, cut up like a jigsaw puzzle. She was trying to put her vehicle into reverse gear and back out. Later we found out that the woman was completely intoxicated (not a big surprise). She had blacked out and driven her truck across three lanes of traffic, over a huge divider, and then through the backyard fence. She came barreling into my bedroom by penetrating first a cement wall and then my window.

At first I was angry and wanted retribution. After all, she could have killed me! When I calmed down, I realized how lucky I was to be alive. It was not lost on me that had I not moved my bed hours before the crash, the impact of the truck would without a doubt have killed both Barb and me. As it was, the right side of the woman's truck missed my head by one foot. Had the truck entered my room anyplace else, my life would not have been spared.

I knew that a higher power had once again played a role in saving my life. I was surely protected. Just as in my escape from my potential abductors at age eleven, a clear voice had spoken to me, and I had listened.

I am approached by many parents whose teens are having scary visions or are hearing information in their heads that they know is coming from a source other than themselves. For teens going through this, an understanding parent means everything.

First, validate the teen. Acknowledge what he or she is seeing or hearing. This will help to build trust, which is important in order to start an open, relaxed dialogue. Then discuss what he or she is seeing and/or hearing, and talk about what it might mean. Using some of my earlier tips, try to confirm whether your child has a gift. After all, you don't want to confuse having a gift with having a mental health issue.

Recently I was informed of a teenage girl who was having visions, premonitions of people being hurt or killed. Her visions were very detailed and what she saw in them would later come to pass. The extensive detail and verified outcome were confirmation of her gift. That what she saw in her visions consistently came to pass defied all odds. This is the clearest sign of psychic ability that you can hope for.

The very first thing kids need to know is that the responsibility to save the world does not rest on their shoulders. Having a vision that a bad thing is going to happen does not mean that you also have the responsibility to change the outcome. Sometimes a bad situation isn't supposed to be altered because it exists for a reason.

This does not mean that you can never make a difference. Young psychics, please keep in mind that sometimes we are given the opportunity to intervene and prolong someone's life.

Say you have a vision that your father is going to be in a car accident, and in the vision he's wearing a red shirt and carrying his golf clubs. You wake up the next morning and your dad is on his way out the door wearing a red shirt and carrying his golf clubs.

Stop him! Explain your dream and ask him to wait awhile or even change his plans. You may be receiving a form of intervention from the other side.

If, on the other hand, in your vision you see a bridge in Tibet being blown up, it's probably out of your hands. Ask a higher power to please lend a gentle hand to those on that bridge who need positive energy. Don't internalize a vision and let it take a toll on you physically

Often young psychics aren't listened to by the proper authorities. The parents of a psychic might try contacting law enforcement if a vision is extraordinarily detailed or significant and explaining that the child had a "dream" (this is a safer term than "vision").

They can explain that the child saw something happen and it would make the child feel a whole lot better if an officer could just check it out.

Many police officers are parents and are usually happy to put a child's mind at ease. Who knows, maybe your child's vision will help somebody, and if not, your child will have at least expressed the information and will feel better. Visions that aren't shared build up in the system, causing stress. Always encourage expression.

For what it's worth, even well-seasoned forensic psychics who have detailed information on terrorist attacks and murders are often ignored by law enforcement. The authorities have a tough time determining who is legitimate and who is wasting their time. Tell your child not to take it personally if his or her information is ignored. It happens to the best of us. This doesn't mean all law enforcement agencies turn a blind eye to psychics, but many still do.

Teens need to ask their guides to not give them more than they can handle. We are provided what we can handle, and sometimes a little more. If it becomes too much, we have to ask our guides to limit what we are exposed to and remove some of the weight that's causing us to feel burdened.

As for the girl with the premonitions, my best advice to her parents was to determine whether the maimings and killings she saw were in any way preventable. For instance, could she tell who the people in the visions were? Did she get extremely specific names or addresses? Such information could be used to forewarn the police. There was no guarantee that the police would listen, but the girl with the information could sleep at night knowing that she had shared her information.

Of course, we must always remember to use discretion. Only share information if it's specific. Psychics have to be careful about unloading on people to make ourselves feel better. It has to be done in the receiver's best interest, not ours. If it's not in the receiver's best interest, ask your guides to relieve you of the information, write it in your journal if needed, and let it go.

Only contact authorities with information that they can check out and that is useful in prevention or conviction. Everything else is useless to them. If there isn't enough detailed information to establish a crime's timing or the identity of the person involved, then the information is not enough for any intervention.

If you bug the police too often with every

little feeling that you get, they will start to not listen to you. You will be branded a wacko psychic and you will lose all credibility with law enforcement. You want to keep this door open in case you find that you really can help solve a crime.

Remember that not all psychics want to help solve crimes, which is fine. This segment is for the ones who crave to be involved in forensics. You have to fine-tune your skills to make a difference, but you can do it.

And sometimes you have to let go of information and ask a higher power to take care of the person in question. We are only human and can only do so much for others.

Teen psychics must learn to keep their guides in check. I tell my guides not to allow any negative or mischievous energy to come into contact with me. Guides are very accommodating and will act in your best interest. Parents, you can ask your own guides to watch over your children; I do. I know my kids are guided, loved, and protected by my guides as well as by their own.

One way to regain peace is to visualize your heart filled with a radiant white light that expands until it has filled you completely and exits your body through every pore. The white light is there to protect and soothe. This exercise is quite beneficial; I do it myself. Another helpful exercise is to visualize a person on the other side to whom you feel connected. Have that person hold a bucket and place all your problems inside for the spirit to take away. Loved ones on the other side enjoy easing our anxiety. This exercise also strengthens the two-way relationship between those who have passed and those who still remain here.

Teens wanting to sharpen their skills should practice on willing friends and family members, keeping in mind that not all their messages will mean something significant. Sometimes the sitter (the person being read) doesn't expect a serious topic to surface and will not own up to the information. It took me time to realize that if I uncovered something that the sitter wanted to hide, he or she might fib about it.

This was a difficult, disheartening lesson for me, because I would feel so sure that I was right and the sitter would deny it. I hold myself to a high standard. After several instances in which I received third-party verification that I was right, I realized what was happening. Sometimes when I was walking out the door, my client's husband or friend would lean in and tell me that my information was correct.

Now when I feel certain of my information I don't let denial bother me. I let it fuel me to get to the explanation behind my information. Then I let it go. If somebody isn't ready to share something private, that's okay, but don't go see a psychic if you've got something to hide.

Sometimes mediums are shown images that require us to play charades with the other side, and sometimes we misinterpret what we are shown. That is why describing whatever we see to the sitter is important; it's a purer form of relaying a message. It's not as effective for a gifted person to try to rationalize the information that they receive. You don't want to taint the information with inferences of your own.

Teens need to remember not to compare themselves with the psychics portrayed in movies. When I was young I questioned whether I had the gift. I looked at the psychics portrayed in movies, searching for a shred of commonality. I couldn't relate.

I know that the discovery and acceptance of my gift was delayed because I had no role models. I want to let all people know that there are plenty of people in business suits with college degrees who possess psychic and mediumship abilities. There are people from all walks of life. There are doctors, mothers, cashiers, teachers, stockbrokers, musicians, children, who appear to be nothing like one another, yet who have a connection in their ability to communicate with the dead and see things that are yet to come.

If you are a teen with the gift and you don't want to develop it, that is fine. The other side doesn't want to give more than a person can handle. Tuning the other side out takes a little practice, but it can be done. If a person makes a conscious decision and ignores the messages, eventually they should fade and be harder to hear. I don't believe this means that the person no longer has the gift. It is still there; it is just dormant. Turning away from the gift will sometimes leave you with an underlying edgy feeling, as if there is something missing in your life that you can't put your finger on.

The most important thing I can say to gifted children everywhere is what I was dying to hear for so long: "I understand what you are going through, you're not alone, and someday this will all make sense to you."

Chapter 7

Empathy

I had often wondered why I felt so physically edgy when my grandpa's spirit made itself known to me in 1978. As a grown psychic, I know the answer. It wasn't that I was looking at someone whom I just saw buried. It was a physical feeling of sickness. Fellow psychics will relate to this.

When people with heightened sensitivity stand next to sick people, we feel their illness. My great-grandfather had just passed over and I was absorbing the cancer energy that had caused his demise. Whenever I have communication with a spirit who passed from cancer, I get the exact same feeling I got from my great-grandpa twenty-six years ago.

Now that I am older I am more closely attuned to the feeling, and often I will sense that the spirit was eaten up or diseased. I can also sense cancer when I am dealing with a survivor of the illness. Seeing the circumstances surrounding someone's death can validate their presence to loved ones and help us understand their reason for passing.

Ever notice how sometimes you instantly get a good feeling about a person, and while someone else can give you the creeps just as quickly? Some people are good and some are evil; most fall somewhere in between. We tend to use first impressions to determine how much we trust a person. I have found the first impression to be the most accurate one. Don't ever second-guess a strong feeling that you have. Trust your gut.

Psychic activity is nothing new. Many people exercise their "sixth sense" regularly. In everyday life we frequently hear ourselves say we have a hunch about this or a vibe about that. And consider the judges, doctors, mothers, fathers, and so on who use their sixth sense every day.

Some people are better than others at listening to their intuition. They may appear to go through life blessed because everything always works out for them. I believe many of these people are indeed blessed, thanks partly to their willingness to listen to their gut feelings, which help them to make the right choices and to know what or whom to avoid.

Some people choose not to listen to their

gut feelings, so they take the long way, filled with pitfalls. Some people don't trust themselves enough to believe in their own intuition. What a mistake. The voice guiding you wants what is best for you. Listen to it.

Some people save the lives of others by listening to their guides. I am referring to the doctors and nurses who use their intuition and empathy to heal the sick and give patients the best possible care. It may mean running a test for a patient that is atypical just because they are moved to do so, or having a patient stay an extra night at the hospital just in case. There's no real logical reason for the decision; it's simply based on an urgent feeling.

Of course, the majority of medical decisions are based on sound information and experience. I am not dismissing their education. Clearly that's important. I am simply acknowledging that a spiritual contribution often comes through in their work.

If you happen to be in the medical field, please remember to take time for yourself. When you leave the hospital, cleanse yourself of earthbound spirits. People who have endured great physical pain or trauma or who die suddenly are often in shock following their deaths. Sometimes, especially in hospitals, earthbound spirits will attach themselves to people with whom they feel comfortable. Some spirits don't even realize they've died; they think they're simply spending time with their doctor, nurse, or loved one.

Even if you don't think you have any spirits lingering around you, it doesn't hurt to say, "Go to the light and you will find your loved ones waiting for you." This will keep them from hanging around you and weighing you down.

Also remember to not be too hard on yourself when you have done your best and your patient dies anyway. As I stated earlier, sometimes it's just not in our hands.

Law enforcement is another field in which people act on hunches and gut feelings. People in this field tend to take their work home with them, because they are constantly around criminals and toxic entities. If you work in law enforcement, you need to remember that all the negative energy you absorb can take a toll on your health. You must remember to take time for yourself to focus on happy, positive things.

Of course, that advice goes for anyone who lets the stresses of life get to them. For all those with stressful, high-pressure jobs that are seemingly without end (yes, that includes motherhood), it is important to take care of yourself.

Chapter 8

Painful Living, Peaceful Good-byes

One of my most memorable experiences with the other side took place in May 2000 while I was in Washington, D.C., for a conference. The many striking monuments mesmerized me and I was enjoying all the important sights in the area. I have always had an interest in the history of the United States and had especially wanted to visit the Vietnam Veterans Memorial, so Joe and I set off to do just that.

We walked down the path, taking in the black marble memorial wall. We sat on a bank overlooking the Reflecting Pool while I shared with my husband what I saw. Two apparitions of American soldiers were at the edge of the pool, one kneeling and one standing. The kneeling soldier was closer to me, no more than twenty feet away; his gun lay on the ground next to him.

I pointed to the area where the soldier knelt and began describing the scene to my husband, when the soldier quickly turned around; he realized that I was talking about him. The earthbound spirit approached me and waved his hand vigorously in front of my face. At this point he was no more than a few inches away.

I addressed him: "Yes, I can see you."

As soon as the words rolled out of my mouth, the soldier, whom I will call Sarge since he was a sergeant, started showing me what had happened to him in Vietnam. It haunted him still.

He was showing me the images as if I were watching a home movie. I saw a thatched hut with a woman inside. Sarge was behind a tree or shrubbery on a small embankment looking down at her. The woman was Vietcong. She had been setting up American soldiers to be ambushed and killed. Sarge was to throw a grenade into her hut and put an end to the "enemy."

He was a good soldier. He wanted to help win the war for his country, which meant that he had to carry out his orders. He saw killing the enemy as saving his friends and comrades from certain death. While the grenade was mid-flight, Sarge heard a baby cry. The baby must have belonged to the Vietcong woman. The hut, the Vietcong woman, and the baby were blown up.

Sarge was beside himself. He was going to war to be a good American, but to him kids were off limits. This was one thing for which he could never forgive himself. Sarge was so overcome by grief that he put himself in the line of fire while in combat. He could not live with being responsible for the death of an innocent child. He figured that since his life was no longer worth anything (as he saw it), then at the very least he could maybe save one of his buddies by trading in his own life. Sarge was successful in getting himself killed.

I was advised by my guides to tell him what he needed to hear. I looked at him as I tried to regain my composure and said, "I forgive you, we all forgive you, and we know that you didn't mean to hurt that baby."

Sarge's young face, wrenched by pain, suddenly relaxed and his skin developed a golden glow. I had been able to do for Sarge what he couldn't do for himself: provide forgiveness. Sarge smiled and stepped back. At the same time, shadowy figures of his family, friends, and fellow soldiers who had waited a long time for Sarge were there to "take him home."

Although Sarge was a soldier, he was also

a sensitive young man with a lot of questions about right and wrong. I haven't shared his story so that others could sit in judgment of him; this isn't about the war or the taking of a life. I have shared the story so that others might learn to forgive themselves for their own mistakes in life, realizing that when we die we carry over our regrets. Forgiveness is not always easy, but it is vital to our existence.

Sarge gave me his rank and his full name. My husband and I looked him up in the book of names at the monument and he was there. And in case you are wondering, his name was not common, like Smith or Jones. I will not disclose it, out of respect for his surviving family.

I think it's important to share Sarge's story with others who have lost family members, friends, and other important loved ones in war. I want people to know that when they talk to the spirits of loved ones or visit memorials of our veterans, those on the other side hear their words.

Also, many of the young men who went to war carry heavy burdens with them. What matters is that we remember that many soldiers have paid a high price for our free country and they did it with love for us. This was one of the most amazing experiences I have ever had, and I am grateful I was able to share it with such an incredible spirit.

Many soldiers' spirits remain at the monument. Most of them are not there out of guilt. In essence, they are there out of their own pride in dying for their country and, as they saw it, for their family's security. The soldiers on the other side enjoy seeing people come to pay tribute to them, and they especially love seeing their surviving buddies come to the memorial. Some soldiers can't believe that such monuments were erected just for them (they're humble). I saw many spirits walking in the area of the Vietnam Memorial and strolling alongside the Reflecting Pool. They are all around us and continue to share moments with us all. I will never forget my encounter with Sarge on that hot day in May.

I had intended to have this chapter be limited to my experience with Sarge. However, I told Joe that somehow it didn't seem finished, and that I would wait to see what event would complete it.

Six months after I first worked on this chapter, history was made when America was attacked on September 11, 2001. Nineteen Arab terrorists hijacked four commercial planes and wreaked havoc on our country. We all cried as we watched people desperately searching for their missing loved ones at Ground Zero in New York. These were no ordinary tears that we cried. We were a united front, crying for people we had never met before. The collective sadness and the extent of our loss was overwhelming.

I am not an overtly emotional woman. My best friend says I seem to be the emotional equivalent of a man, meaning I am uncomfortable crying and showing extreme emotion. I feel very deeply for people, but I keep my feelings inside.

I remember sitting on the edge of the couch, my eyes fixed on the TV, staring at the aftermath of the World Trade Center and the Pentagon disasters. I could not mentally digest that a group of terrorists had tried to kill our president along with thousands of others. When "The Star Spangled Banner" was played at the changing of the guards at Buckingham Palace, my heart swelled with pride. I also felt love for our friends in other countries who shared our sense of loss.

People often ask me whether all people have some good in them, deep down. My answer is no. I believe that all children have good inside them that only needs to be elicited. I realize that medical exceptions may exist, but I am talking about the majority.

But adults are different. Somewhere in between childhood and adulthood we can lose our sense of conscience if we're not careful.

Osama bin Ladin truly scares me, because he's a lunatic. I believe bin Ladin is someone we can't even begin to reason with. He comes from a completely different place, one we can never truly understand. What a wonderful difference he could have made in this world if he had put all that money and effort into something positive.

I want to tell the families and friends who lost loved ones in this cowardly terrorist attack that the victims were not alone when they passed. Their family members on the other side were there when called, and they sheltered those who were about to join them. From the other side, the mothers, fathers, grandparents and others took those loved ones home quickly and lovingly. In some cases, intervention was possible. That is why some people were saved, such as those who were late to work that day due to traffic jams or other delays.

As I watched the towers fall, I had a vision. I saw a woman in a blazer and skirt;

she was huddled on the ground next to a desk. She was scared and she was praying as the building crumbled around her. I started to feel anger that she had to die this way. In that moment I saw the strongest, kindest, golden-white light descend through the ceiling above her and as it lowered, settling over her, it took the shape of a hand. In that swift and loving gesture, the woman's fear was removed and she knew that she was no longer alone.

There are psychics who wouldn't write about such a thing because it touches on religion. I don't care; the hand wasn't wearing a religious symbol or preaching. The hand was that of a god whose only intention was to show some level of mercy. The hand of this higher power covered people, shielding some of them from certain death. The same hand swiftly carried over those that he needed to call home. We might not understand why certain people lived and others died, but that doesn't mean there isn't some sort of plan.

I know that I wasn't the only person who wanted to jump into my television set and help New York's police and firefighters sift through the rubble. That rubble contained our brothers and sisters. We are forever changed. The terrorists tried to defeat

America and failed. They did succeed, however, in uniting the rest of us as never before.

God bless the brave people who wrestled the terrorists on flight 93 and saved countless lives. If I live to be a hundred, their actions will always move me to tears. I am in awe. Thank you to our pilots, flight attendants, passengers, firefighters, police officers, and all those who lost their lives that day. Thank you for gracing the world with your presence. We are humbled by your bravery and by the magnitude of what you were forced to endure. They are beyond words.

The attacks changed America in many ways. Some of them are blessings in disguise. For example, many people who have lost their jobs are asking themselves if they want to explore a different field that might be more spiritually fulfilling. I have family members who have been affected by the layoffs. It's amazing to see people who were once climbing the white-collar ladder of success and are now considering firefighting because they want to fill the voids in their souls.

September 11 has made people ask what is really important in life and how they can make a difference. It has brought about much soul-searching. This is an opportunity for people to realize that they can change the course of their lives. It's never too late. To me, the worst thing you can do with your life is squander it.

Children have so many dreams, and they find laughter and joy in so many ways. Sometimes adults get so bogged down in making their credit card payments that they forget there is more to life. Sometimes we forget that we can become whatever we want and our age shouldn't be an issue.

Can you imagine if we didn't have people willing to go out on a limb to create change in our world? If we didn't have people who believe in joy? We wouldn't have places like Disneyland. Talk shows exploring spirituality and personal happiness wouldn't exist. My best advice for those looking for fulfillment? Strike out on your own, and be able to look back on your life and say, "I did that." When a good idea pops into your head, don't dismiss it. Dare to care about what matters to you, and be strong enough to stand your ground against naysayers.

I look at my own life and I feel so fulfilled and blessed in doing what I do. I am under constant scrutiny, always being asked, "Do you really believe that people still exist after they die?"

I always answer, "Oh, yes. I'm one of the few people in the world who is sure they do."

Often I hear "I am a skeptic; I don't believe in an afterlife." My answer is skeptics will know for sure after they die. It's true!

No matter how many slams I receive, I will gladly endure them. They're a small price to pay for such a blessed life.

Chapter 9

Little Things

I have included this chapter to share with you some of the little things that we human beings tend to take for granted in life. These are the same things that we cherish most after we lose a loved one. It is often the little things that poignantly connect us to the other side. Being able to provide the name of a deceased loved one is good, but sentimental details are more personal and confirm the authenticity of the connection to someone on the other side.

I realized after countless readings that the little things are important because what may seem insignificant to most people is a priceless, soothing detail to another. My clients have contributed the following readings so that you can share their feelings from revisiting loved ones who have passed away. Each reading has touched me and taught me something new about being a medium.

Occasionally the information I communicate to my client doesn't make sense to him at the time of the reading and he looks quite perplexed. Usually within a couple of weeks I receive a telephone call or card from that client coupled with a story that sheds light on the previously unfamiliar details. Some new experience or discovery has made the information I gave pertinent.

In other situations, the intensity of a good reading can mean that it takes time for the client to process all the information being received. I've gotten first names, middle names, last names, cities, car models, favorite food dishes, you name it. After all the efforts I made to give the most impressive information possible, what I found mattered most was the small stuff. One of the many lessons that I've learned from the other side is that it's the little things that are powerful enough to tear down the toughest walls of disbelief.

✦ *Holding Hands with the Other Side*

I once did a reading for a beautiful, effervescent sixteen-year-old girl, whom I'll call Lisa; Lisa had recently lost her best friend, whom I'll call Kim, in a horrible car accident, and she needed closure surrounding

Kim's death. Kim came through and shared many messages that were significant to Lisa; among other things, she talked about a pinball machine that they had played often, and told Lisa about a so-called friend who didn't have Lisa's best interests at heart.

Lisa wanted to be sure of my ability, so she threw out names and then asked me to comment on the people. I didn't mind being tested. I prefer to receive limited information from clients, so the impact of the information I give them is greater. And I enjoy a challenge, as long as it's not delivered out of anger. I was on target with the people Lisa tested me on, but Kim didn't feel that Lisa was getting the full message. Kim then provided me with information that was intended to get Lisa's attention. I turned to her and said, "Lisa, who is number eleven? I am being shown a sports jersey with the number eleven on the back."

Lisa's paused and said, "That's me. I am number eleven on my high school basketball team."

So two best friends who had done everything together until parted by death were able to reconnect. I explained to Lisa that the information was given to me by Kim in order to get her full attention so that she would take the information to heart. Kim is still watching out for Lisa and loving her. Lisa had no doubt that Kim was with us that afternoon and is still walking through life with her.

✦ Mom

I have many clients who have lost a parent. It's hard to let go of parents. Either you were lucky in having a good relationship and now you miss them, or they were never there for you and you need a connection to experience closure. It is completely understandable that either of these are painful enough to require closure.

Rick is a burly man whose caring, good-hearted nature drew me in immediately. He appeared at my door cheerful but hesitant. As we sat down for his one-hour reading, he told me that his mother had just died. He was having a hard time dealing with her loss because he was a long haul driver and was on I-80 in Nebraska at the time that she passed.

I said, "Your mother is making my head hurt from both the inside and outside. Does that make sense to you? Like maybe she had an aneurysm and her head hit a table or something when she fell."

"Yes, she had a stroke while she was in her bathroom, and hit her head on the sink when she fell," he said.

"Well, she doesn't want her husband to be blamed; she insists he's not at fault."

Rick mentioned that some family members had blamed his father.

"I keep seeing a roulette table." (I was hoping he wouldn't take this badly. Sometimes, something comes out in a reading that a client might find offensive — like an affair or compulsive gambling — especially if the subject is his mother.) "Did she want to go to Las Vegas, or had she been there recently?"

He looked stunned. "Yes!"

Rick explained that his mother had just returned from Las Vegas the day she died. She had put down her suitcase, walked into her bedroom-bathroom, suffered a stroke, and died. Rick's dad was at work at the time and when he returned home it seemed as if no one was home. He opened the door to his bedroom and noticed that the lights were out, but his wife wasn't in bed. So he went into the kitchen to fix something to eat and decided to watch TV while waiting for her to return. He hadn't realized that his wife was on the bathroom floor, unable to call out for help.

126

Because of this, Rick had feelings of turmoil attached to his mother's passing. His mother was setting the record straight from the other side by relieving her family of the guilt and frustration that burdened them.

"Rick, did your mother have a round table with a bowl of fruit on it?"

"Yes, and now I have it."

"Your mother still sits there. It's your daily time together, she says."

Tears formed in his eyes. Rick's mom then referred to a woman named Susan; she wanted Rick to know that Susan and she were together. I then asked Rick to call Susan's mother (if she was open to hearing from the other side) and tell her that her daughter was okay and that she was with his mother.

Rick wasn't fully aware of how significant this message was at the time but he was happy to hear Susan's name mentioned. When he left that day, he said he felt a great weight had been lifted off his shoulders.

He called me the next day to tell me that he had contacted Susan's mother, who lives in Florida. He told her about his reading with me and passed on the news that Susan was with his mom and was very happy. She started crying and said she had been thinking about her Susie all week: The next day was the anniversary of her death. She said that she had been talking to Susan because she missed her so much and had hoped that Susan could hear her. Susan definitely answered that question.

Rick's phone call gave Susan's mother confirmation that her daughter was still with her. It was no coincidence that Rick's phone call came the day before the anniversary of Susan's death.

Rick and his mother are connected in life and in the afterlife. So are Susan and her mother. The mother-child bond can never be broken.

✦ *I Believe*

I never know quite what to expect at a group session. Sometimes the participants have so much in common that we realize that there is a running group theme. On the flip side, occasionally I will meet a participant who isn't sure about being there but has committed to at least observing the group. Without fail, the observer is pulled in when a visitor from the other side insists on sending a message.

One story that comes to mind is that of George, a handsome, well-manicured man with silver in his hair. As I shook his hand, George smiled and said, "I have to tell you, I am a skeptic."

"That's all right," I said. "Everyone should approach this experience with open eyes. Don't force the information to fit."

He assured me that he would not. It didn't take long for George's visitor from the other side to make himself known. I told George that his grandfather was coming through and he asked which one.

"Your grandfather is showing me New York City, so he was either from New York or it was significant to him," I said.

George thought for a moment and then said, "I don't think so."

I repeated my advice about not forcing anything.

"Oh wait, my grandfather came to this country through Ellis Island."

I described his grandfather and mentioned his grandfather's fondness for suspenders. The suspenders were significant to George and he was pleased. I gave him more information about his family and elaborated on his grandfather before finishing his reading.

"Everything you said was right on except the part about my grandfather playing checkers; he didn't play checkers," he said.

I explained that I give what I get and that maybe it would make sense to him later. Two weeks later I received a call from George's fiancée, who had accompanied George to the group session. She said that they were out shopping and came upon a store window with a display that included a checkerboard.

She saw George staring at the checkerboard and asked where his mind had wandered. George turned to her and said, "My grandfather use to take me to the park when I was a little boy and he'd give me fifteen cents to get lost so that he could play checkers."

George was stunned to realize that he had long forgotten this part of his youth. Both the reading and the checkerboard in the store had triggered his memory recall. I have no doubt that George's grandfather played a part in helping him to put together the pieces. His grandfather succeeded in convincing George that he was, is, and always will be with him. George later sent me a lovely card that said, "I believe." Thank you, George. It means more than you know.

Sometimes people like to make my group sessions a family outing. A striking young woman named Barbara showed up with her sister, Jen, and their aunt for a group session. During that session I was distracted by Barbara's grandfather (who was deceased), who insisted on my conveying images to his girls. I told Barbara and her family that her grandfather was talking about bedtime stories:

"He says he would read you fairy tales and he's showing me a castle on a hill with a winding road leading up to the castle."

You could have knocked all three of them over with a feather. Barbara shared that on the way over she had been thinking about her grandpa and how he'd read her bedtime stories when she was little. She had told her aunt, who was in the car with her, that she wanted Grandpa to come through and talk about the bedtime stories that he used to read to her and Jen when they were little. She and her aunt fondly reminisced and agreed that the bedtime stories would convince them that Grandpa was around them.

Barbara's sister Jen, who had driven her car separately, was the skeptic of the bunch, but her jaw dropped as well. She said that on the way over she had told her grandpa that if he was there with her he should tell Allison about the fairy tales he used to read to her when she was little. She specifically requested "Cinderella." Jen was thrilled and knew that her grandpa was there for her that day with his book in hand. All three women had the same sweet connection with Grandpa, and they all knew he was listening to them on the way to the group session.

✦ *Easter Lily*

Like most people, I have a social life. On the weekends, I often find that business and pleasure blend. It was a sunny Saturday afternoon, and some of my girlfriends and I indulged by eating lunch out for a change. We later stopped by Champions for a cocktail. I only get to do this once in a great while, so I was ready to listen to the jukebox and unwind. My best friend, Stacey, had been chatting with the lady bartender when suddenly she came flying back to our table.

"Allison! This poor girl, you have to talk to her. She really needs your input."

I was pretty relaxed, so I said, "Sure, tell her to come over. I'll talk to her."

Our bartender approached me. "Hi! I'm

Kim. I hope I'm not bothering you."

I assured her that everything was fine. We briefly talked about a health concern of hers. Then Kim said, "I really wonder about a friend of mine who died. I hope she's with me."

With great confidence I said, "Oh, she's with you. She's showing me an Easter lily. So she's making a reference to April. Did she die in April? Was her birthday in April?"

(Here's an example of how crucial it is for me to illustrate what I am being shown by the other side. This advice is important for people with psychic instincts to remember: Describe everything you're seeing; it will help you to read your sitter better. The information that we get isn't always what we think it is. Sometimes the sitter is helpful in the "charades game" with the afterlife. We are only messengers; sometimes we need clarity from the person sitting in front of us.)

"My mother's name is April," Kim replied. Her friend hadn't been referring to the month of April, but rather was giving me the name April. I then turned to Kim and said, "Your friend is now making reference to May by spelling M-A-Y."

Kim laughed and said, "May is my middle name. I was named after my godmother." Those were the only names and/or months that I gave her. We talked for another few minutes, and then she went back to work with a new sense of peace.

✦ Meeting of the Minds

On one occasion I had the opportunity to sit down with a fantastic married couple, Carol and Randy, for an informal reading when my husband and I were out to dinner with them. My favorite skeptic, Randy, looked at me and said, "What's my lucky number?"

I shot back with six.

"She's right; it's six! I played a game and won with the lucky number six. It's been my lucky number ever since."

We all laughed and they joked about taking me to Las Vegas.

Then Carol asked, "Hey, Allison! When my friend falls in love, what's the name of the woman he will fall for?"

"Ann."

Her jaw dropped and she shared that they had just set Randy's friend up with a coworker of hers. Her name? Anna.

Later I was told that the newly introduced couple in question had a very passionate first date. Good for them! After that, Randy always had a question for me, but he no longer questioned my abilities.

Randy died suddenly in November 2002, the victim of a massive heart attack. I now get to hear from my favorite skeptic from the other side.

✦ Shooting Star

I love to give people signs to look for from the deceased so they will know their loved ones are present. I understand the importance of this because most people cannot see spirits. It's good personal verification. I did a reading for the widow of a pilot who died in a plane crash. She referred her sister-in-law to me for a reading weeks later. Two very special things happened during that reading. One occurred when Chris, the sister of the deceased pilot, asked me if I could tell her about the question he asked her during their last conversation.

I told her that he asked her if she'd be the godmother of his child.

Chris was very quiet and asked me to repeat what I had just said. I obliged. That was, in fact, her brother's last question to her. My focus was right on. Working in the

University of Arizona Human Energy Systems laboratory, where I studied, has really made me comfortable with answering questions like this. Sometimes in pushing yourself to the limit you can exceed your own expectations.

The second gift to Chris from her brother was his sign. He said she would know that he was around her when she sees a shooting star.

Later I received an e-mail from Chris. She was awestruck. She told me that when I told her the sign was a shooting star she didn't know what to think. She had never seen a shooting star and she couldn't imagine when the heck she'd see one.

She went on to describe what had happened over Thanksgiving. Chris was sitting in the living room playing with her niece/goddaughter. The little girl was playing with a magic wand that had a star at the end of it. She looked at her aunt and was preparing to throw it to her.

"Aunt Chris," she called, "look at the shooting star!"

Chris immediately remembered what her brother had said: "When you see the shooting star, think of me and I'll be there."

I found this greatly symbolic because her brother sent the message through his daughter, who is a part of him, a part that Chris can still hold. She knows that her brother was spending that day with his family and that he will always be close by.

Take the time to think about the little things that mean the most to you. What do you really treasure about those that you love? If you ever need to be reminded that there's life after death, revisit this chapter and know that there is more to life than what we see on the surface.

Chapter 10

Gifted

I am asked all the time what it is like to see dead people. I have decided to address this in my book so that others can understand my life and other psychics' lives a little better. First of all, let me say that being a psychic-medium is truly a gift. It is part of me and I would not relinquish the ability if I could. I try to have fun with it. I have a T-shirt that I sometimes wear to group sessions: "I see dead people" it reads. My clients appreciate my humor.

On the flip side, being a psychic is no easy life. Like anything else, it has pros and cons. I hate the stereotypes associated with it, and the image many people have of a frizzy-haired, talon-fingered, incense-burning weirdo. Being a medium is both a blessing and a challenge.

Imagine if everything that ever happened in your life was under a microscope. Most people will never know what it feels like to be called the Antichrist or to be judged before you are ever met. And then there is the assumption that people like me should always be ready to help or entertain.

Like those in other professions, we don't always want to talk shop or be asked for advice when we are out having a good time. We love to go to social engagements and simply be guests like everyone else. I enjoy occasions when I can just blend in and be normal. You want help? Call me on Monday.

As for the calling I have, even when I was young I asked what was so amazing out there that I was being drawn to. I could not define it, but I could see it, feel it, and hear it. I've read that other mediums have had similar experiences in childhood. It comforts me to know that there are at least a few others out there who know how I feel.

✦ *No Real Role Models*

Since my parents were divorced, I saw my dad every Saturday. He would pick me up and take me to a movie and lunch. I enjoyed our time together. I am sure that I saw every movie made from the mid-1970s to the late 1980s. I was always curious about ghosts and loved movies about the other side.

Unfortunately, I could not relate to the psychics in most movies. They seemed too odd or New Age (no offense to New Agers; I just couldn't relate). I didn't see anyone who seemed like me. Were there lots of young people with the gift, or was it like a driver's license, so that you had to be a certain age to get it? I needed more information about the other side.

It was seldom that I saw a movie about kids with the gift. There was an occasional film involving kids who could see a spirit, but they were never defined as gifted. They were in an isolated situation, and after the wronged spirit received closure, it was implied that the sightings ceased. With that kind of portrayal, seeing ghosts seemed more like a fluke than a gift.

When I was a child my favorite spirit flick was a Disney Sunday Night Movie about a glass doll in an attic and a little girl's spirit that needed closure. The premise was that living children were trying to find out what had happened to a little girl who had died many years before. They were trying to bring her closure through their communication with her and to uncover the circumstances surrounding her death. The children could both see and hear the little girl on the other side, and to me this made sense.

The best part of the movie was that the kids who could see the girl's spirit were normal kids, not portrayed as nuts or weirdos. The movie was haunting, and it made me excited about interacting with the other side. I loved it. And I was continually being introduced to scenarios that would one day be commonplace for me. My spirit was being fueled to connect with the other side.

I also found myself drawn to study the criminal mind throughout my childhood. Although I didn't realize what I was doing until I was an adult, I watched anything and everything on TV that covered actual homicides. My mind would receive information that filled in gaps surrounding murders, such as pictures of the perpetrator, weapons, names, places, and motives. Later in life, I would learn that I have a knack for profiling criminals. My specialty is tapping into the human mind for this purpose. More specifically, I can determine what a particular person's motive is, his emotion or lack of emotion, and the result of his impulses.

✦ *My Gift*

The idea of the unknown is an easy target for people who would rather believe that when we die we become worm food. Believing this relieves you of any spiritual or personal reflection, which can be painful. Also, people with this mind-set tend to not be very worried about the ramifications of the way they treat others, and they're comfortable with this. I was on a show once and I had a well-known moron (who shall remain nameless) say to me, "Well, I believe that there are spirits, but I sure as hell can't hear them or talk to them!"

My response was "Well, duh! That's because you're not a medium."

Is that such a hard concept for people to grasp? If we could all hear and see spirits, we'd all be mediums. To me it's no different from being born with some other significant gift. No matter how many singing lessons I have I will never sound like Celine Dion; not even close. No matter how hard I study I will never have the mind of Albert Einstein. No matter how hard some people try, they will never see or talk to spirits. That's okay; that's what makes the world so interesting.

To help people to better understand mediums, I'm addressing some misconceptions about us. Sometimes a medium might appear cold or aloof. Mediums often find themselves withdrawing emotionally in a reading, to ensure that they can deliver all the information from the other side and bring closure to their client. For me, it's sometimes a struggle to keep from getting pulled into the emotion of a reading. But I know that once I start getting emotional my concentration is gone, and this can weaken the clarity of my connection to the other side.

The appearance of arrogance can also be a misconception. When mediums get a feeling for their accuracy levels, they know when they are right on target and so they feel confident. Since the rest of the world questions us, mediums learn quickly to either stand behind their information or keep their mouths closed. Many people misjudge mediums who believe in their own accuracy, deeming them arrogant, when actually these mediums had to become their own biggest believers in order to persevere.

Younger mediums need to be confident in their information but remember to be humble and to appreciate that sitters are sharing their personal lives. Mediums are simply messengers, not miracle workers.

Our main goal is to help and guide others, not to show off.

I find solace in my family, the people to whom I've given closure, the other people with my gift, my guides, and my own sense of humor. If you're a psychic who is in the closet, let me just say that you can try to ignore your gift, but embracing it feels much more natural.

Remember that people can't go to school to become psychic, and you can't buy psychic skill, it's a gift. Everyone has a unique knack for something in life; mine is talking to people who are deceased, and I like it. The dearly departed don't have all the hang-ups that the living have and I find them easier to talk to.

When I am preparing for a private reading, I know the other side is churning around me when my hands quickly become freezing. I refer to this as holding hands with the other side. It has taken me a while, but I'm used to it now. I just stick my hands on my husband, who warms them up for me. (He's multitalented.)

Finding a mentor or a psychic whom you can relate to helps a lot. I was fortunate enough to have a mentor, Catherine, a psychic-medium-astrologer who is top-notch at exercising her gift. In her, I found a teacher who broke the stereotypical mold of a psychic and enabled me to become comfortable with my gift. Not all psychics are creepy-looking women with crystal balls who go into scary trances and eat all-natural foods.

Most of us are pretty normal. I love Dr Pepper; I drink it by the bucketful. Some people who are more spiritually inclined tell me that it impairs my psychic ability. I actually tried drinking a lot of soda to make the spirits go away. I can assure you, it didn't work for me.

In addition to drinking gallons of Dr Pepper, I like to wear suits, eat junk food, crank up my music, and watch scary movies (because they're not real). I don't spend my days meditating for hours. Despite its potential usefulness, I am far too impatient for it. Usually I do a five-minute quickie meditation asking my guides to bring through the information from the other side loud and clear and in the best interest of my client.

I went to school to be a prosecuting attorney. I was an intern in homicide at a local district attorney's office. I was trying to ignore my gift and go down the path more easily traveled, where you don't have to fight people for common respect. I hid my gift and lived a parallel life with another agenda, but the gift is part of me and I must honor it. My guides tried to tell me that I had a different path to travel, that I wasn't going to be a lawyer, but I wouldn't listen.

I am sharing this with those of you who feel that life is trying to take you in one direction and you want to go in another. I had my fingers in my ears and I was humming a tune to drown my guides out. I jumped through all the hoops and I took my LSATs because I was going to law school, darn it! Over a six-month period, I had more road-blocks thrown up in front of me than I could jump. Finally I looked at my husband and I said, "I don't think I'm suppose to go to law school." Joe had been wondering how long it would take me to figure that out.

I have come to terms with the fact that there isn't a big demand for psychic prose-cuting attorneys; the politics are compli-cated, and I stand out too much. So I will listen to my calling and take on as many challenges as possible, testing my ability to the limit.

One of the downfalls of being a psychic is that you're expected to know absolutely everything. Most people have no understanding of reading energy.

Can you imagine what it's like living as a perceived know-it-all? If your dishwasher breaks, you're asked, "Didn't you see that coming?" If your child slips and falls, you hear, "Why didn't you know ahead of time; aren't you a psychic?"

First of all, it can take a lot of energy to turn up our volume, so we aren't always paying attention; we are busy living, and we are only human. Also, psychics don't see everything. Yes, we have a sixth sense, but our other five senses are fallible, so why is our sixth sense not permitted any leeway?

Psychics can fall prey to all the normal human foibles. For instance, we have all had our eyes play tricks on us, where we think we see someone we know and then find out that it wasn't who we thought it was after all. Or sometimes we don't hear someone clearly when they speak to us. Often we think we hear our name being called and then find out that it was just voices on the television downstairs. Or we can't remember where we put something.

Sometimes the human senses mislead us. People frequently will confuse smells or make an incorrect guess about an ingredient in a friend's recipe. This can happen with the sixth sense, too. Once I saw a client standing next to a "For Sale" sign in my vision. I asked her if she was selling her house. She said no. But I kept seeing her over and over again, next to the "For Sale" sign. Finally I asked her, "Are you thinking of becoming a real estate agent and selling houses for a living?" She said yes, she had been thinking lately of becoming a real estate agent.

"It's being made very clear to me that this is the direction for you to go," I told her. When a vision keeps coming back, the other side is emphasizing something significant, like a person's direction in life. In the vision, my client looked extremely happy and well off, which illustrates success to me. Psychics have to be careful deciphering what they see; it can be tricky. Trial and error is the only way for mediums to learn. Once we've experienced, say, the feeling for a heart attack, we recognize it the next time. Mediums need to experience the various types of death and emotions in order to have a reference to draw on to give a fantastic reading. But it takes practice.

I once had a young woman in her twenties ask me to tell her about her health. I looked at her and said I felt a problem with her muscles and joints. I was being given carpal tunnel syndrome as an example of debilitation in her hands. I said that I didn't feel the intense effects would occur just yet. She told me that she had multiple sclerosis. I asked her if she was in remission, and she said she was.

I hadn't read anyone with MS before, so I didn't know the feeling associated with it. I was right about her symptoms but failed to identify the illness. I knew that her ailment was not severe at present and that she had some time before it would become challenging. Now I can recognize that feeling. Life experience increases a medium's ability to read because she can understand what she senses better through repetition.

There are occasions when psychic-mediums just *know* without having to concentrate, or when we are overwhelmed by a persistent spirit who wants our attention badly. Sometimes I'll have a spirit scream a name in my ear until I repeat his message; sometimes the desire to get through outweighs good etiquette. We get what we get; it depends on the strength and clarity of the energy on the other side, our ability to receive the message, and the willingness of the loved one to whom we convey the message.

Sometimes a living loved one is looking to hear a particular word. Despite highly specific information given to them, they feel disappointed or annoyed if the reading doesn't go according to their own agenda. Instead, the reading follows the agenda of their loved one on the other side.

Look at it from a spirit's perspective. Imagine you desperately want to talk to someone whom you have waited ten years to talk to. You only have thirty minutes to say everything that you want to say to them. You want to fill a void and be acknowledged as being with them in their present life. This may be your only shot at letting your loved one know how you feel. What would be important? What would you say? That you love them, that you are sorry, their name, names of people who are with them, memories or objects that have emotional value.

You probably wouldn't be worried about a code word; you'd be too busy expressing emotion, whether it was love, happiness, or regret. You'd want to touch your loved one's heart. So if you're lucky enough to make contact with a loved one, hear their message and allow them to touch you. Let go of your agenda.

✦ "Psychic" Is a Dirty Word

One day I found myself on a show where a poll was taken of the audience to see who did or didn't believe that mediums can communicate with the dead. The host said, "Who believes that psychics are frauds, and who's gullible and misguided?"

I couldn't believe he would ask such a leading question to try and sway his audience. I was sitting quietly, waiting to do a taped reading for the show, when the camera crew began mocking the topic of the show. They were making ghost sounds and laughing hysterically. I mentally shut down and decided I didn't care about the reading.

The sitter ended up being skeptical and emotionally closed off anyway. It seemed as if she came in only to prove us wrong. I received confirmation on the two names provided by her father on the other side, but those relatives meant little to her, so she was unimpressed. She didn't take into account that they meant a lot to her father. I also named a hugely important and unique object connected to her father's death, but at that point we were informed our time was up.

Oh well, I thought, at least it's over. I had had only three and a half hours of sleep the night before, because of a five a.m. flight, so I was looking forward to a nap.

Every time the word "psychic" was mentioned at this appearance it was delivered with sneers and contempt, like a dirty word. Anyone who admitted that he believed in psychics was ridiculed and quickly shot down. Such reactions aren't limited to this particular show. That's partly because of people who pass themselves off as psychics to con people out of money. You have to remember that every profession has its share of liars and criminals. Anyone who wants to consult a psychic should ask a friend for a recommendation or ask for references to avoid being conned.

As a medium who had definitely paid her dues, I didn't appreciate being ridiculed by a group of relative strangers. But this experience was a blessing in disguise. Wondering why I bother to be a public figure in this field, I learned a valuable lesson: to not let hostile nonbelievers drive me from my path in life.

As I say, nobody breaks a glass ceiling without being cut.

✦ *What Makes a Skeptic?*

When a skeptic hears the word "psychic," he will usually go on the defensive right away. There is a stigma attached to the word, but I have learned to never be ashamed to own the ability. To see things that most can't or won't is nothing less than a wondrous gift.

There is nothing wrong with being something of a skeptic. Skeptics are on the fence. They aren't sure one way or the other and they're not easily persuaded. If they receive detailed, specific information, they can become believers. If they don't hear what they need to, they continue to have doubts about the afterlife, but remain somewhat open to the possibility. I can understand and wholeheartedly respect their stance. Not only are they entitled to their beliefs, they are wise to have a healthy sense of doubt.

Angry skeptics are a different story. These are people who project their anger stemming from the loss of someone close to them onto issues dealing with the unknown. They tend to have abandonment issues. An angry skeptic can also be a person who feels superior in intelligence to the rest of society, therefore thinking everyone else is dumb or gullible. They also tend to see any sign of emotion as weakness.

They make mediums the target of their anger as they protect the less capable from us. They tend to talk loudly to drown out a medium's response to their question, which was really more a statement, anyway. They tend to make ridiculous arguments against the other side: "I talk to my dead aunt but she doesn't talk back." It never occurs to angry skeptics that they are so closed off that they are incapable of hearing those who have passed on. Plus, they obviously lack mediumistic energy. The entire population isn't expected to hear the dead.

Angry skeptics tend to present arguments such as "Mediums are too general." Okay, sometimes people die of heart attacks and some are named Michael, like my dad. Should a medium not acknowledge the spirit of a loved one because his death wasn't unique enough or his name is too common? Mediums acknowledge whoever comes through, and it would be stupid of us to ignore a spirit because it doesn't meet with skeptics' approval. The general information has to be delivered; it's a part of the spirit. However, some personally specific information should surface as well.

I came to the realization that I could spend my entire life trying to please difficult people like this, but what a waste of time and energy that would be. Besides, they are a minuscule group. For a long time I felt it necessary to acknowledge angry skeptics personally, to try to make them understand that what mediums do is the most innately human of functions: We connect. But now I ignore these people.

If an angry skeptic won't acknowledge the spiritual aspect of the afterlife and won't acknowledge our scientific approach to the afterlife, then it's his own hang-up. If a person is raising his voice and turning red when talking about life after death, then he needs to assess why he feels so enraged and whether he needs to seek help with issues.

What are angry skeptics so afraid of? That most people do believe in an afterlife and this forces them to acknowledge their life choices? That their words and actions are being witnessed by those they've lost? Angry skeptics are the same people who insisted the world was flat. They are afraid of what they might find if they explore the unknown. Now that healthy skeptics and unhealthy skeptics have been defined, here's to staying healthy!

✦ Boundaries

It's so important for everyone to create boundaries in her life. Here is an example of one that I felt I owed it to myself to draw. Young mediums need to consider what makes them comfortable with their gifts. They are also entitled to establish boundaries and know that they deserve the same courtesy as everyone else.

If I had a quarter for every time I had a person look at me and say, "I am a skeptic, but tell me, how many kids do I have?" or "What am I thinking of right now?"

As if I live simply to provide amusement.

I will not pick lottery numbers for skeptics or entertain them at social gatherings. Skeptics need to remember that mediums are people with lives and we deserve to be treated with respect. It's not necessary to offend us, especially at a social function. I can respect a skeptic not believing in the other side — that's their belief; respect mine.

On the other hand, on many occasions a skeptic has left a reading with an appreciation of the other side and a new outlook on life after death. I find former skeptics to be some of the most emphatic believers in spirits and the idea of eternal existence. People have an idea of what they would

156

have to hear to be convinced that a spirit is communicating with the living. Once a person has heard what they hoped to hear, a weight seems to be lifted from their shoulders; this can be felt by all who witness it.

Also, a person who has had a remarkable reading usually finds a sense of renewed spirituality. They would be very likely to tune out nay-sayers because they have connected with the other side, and this bond is not easily broken.

My gift is used to help people who really need and want closure, people who are inspired to reconnect with a loved one and tie up any loose ends. Some people are in search of guidance or need to know what motivates someone in their life. This allows them to have a clear picture of what they're dealing with so that they can make the best choice for their situation.

I am more than happy to be specific and give compelling information from the other side, but I don't think that mediums owe everybody in the world proof that we exist. I believe there is a higher power, and this higher power didn't create us just to let us die. We are never ending. We are spiritual beings capable of communicating with the spirits of our loved ones even beyond physical death.

Legitimate psychics also have to live with many stigmas. For example, there are a lot of con artists out there who give legitimate mediums a bad name. This irritates me, of course. It's just wrong. Once I had a client ask me if I was going to charge her for lighting candles that would ward off bad spirits. I hadn't heard of this before and I asked her what she was talking about. She told me that she had been to a psychic who had ten- to fifty-dollar candles. The psychic said that these would ward off bad spirits that were causing the difficulty in the client's life.

If you ever go to a psychic and they try to sell you anything by telling you that without it your future is bleak, turn around and walk out immediately. A psychic will occasionally suggest that you burn sage if your home feels negative or if you feel a presence that bothers you, but they in no way should profit from a fifty-cent stick of sage. They might suggest a book, if you inquire about reading material or a source of information. Avoid a psychic who says you will go to hell or never find love, or that anything else terrible will happen, if you don't light a hundred-dollar candle or something of that sort.

Good psychics will not want their clients

to be dependent on them for every move that they make in their lives. We want our clients to pull themselves up by their bootstraps and make the most out of their lives, and, most important, to be happy.

So please remember to not lump all psychics together. If you go to a psychic for a reading and she tells you that your grandma is with you, don't shut down. Ask the medium to tell you about your grandma. You need not offer details about your loved one. Let the medium give the details.

When the reading is over, it's fine to elaborate on the information given to you by the medium. Be very clear that a legitimate medium should have no problem giving you personal details about your deceased loved one. It's what makes us mediums! We can communicate with the dead.

If the medium has provided you with specific details without hints from you, then also accept the generalities that will probably accompany the reading, such as illnesses and heart attacks. If you take the specifics, you have to take the generalities, too. A good medium should be able to put your mind at ease.

If a medium gives you extraordinary personal details, then allow yourself to be touched no matter how skeptical you feel. If you don't, you're doing a disservice to yourself and your loved one. If you are aware that you are feeling emotionally blocked, then accept that you're not ready to be convinced. Timing is important, and some people are just not ready to connect with the afterlife. Don't worry; that's okay.

I know that a lot of skeptics will say that psychics don't want to deal with them because they will reveal our shortcomings. This couldn't be further from the truth. The truth is that skeptics tend to have an energy that is vile and repelling. It doesn't matter what information a psychic comes through with, because this kind of skeptic will deny, deny, deny. For us psychics, spending time with a skeptic like this is like beating our head against a wall, and we will not waste our time or energy on a person like that.

When you go to a reading, by all means don't be a pushover and don't try to force the information given by a psychic to fit your situation; be objective. All I ask is that you be open to receiving messages and remember it's not your agenda, it's what the other side has in mind that will be heard. This doesn't mean that you won't get the information you seek; it means that you will receive a kaleidoscope of information from the other side, so listen carefully.

When I read a client, I try not to edit the information coming through. If the information serves no other purpose than to injure, I have had occasion to hold back, but that's rare. It's not that the spirits intend to hurt the client, but they may have a message to be passed on to another relative and see the opportunity to achieve their goal.

If a spirit did something that he was ashamed of while he was alive and now wants to reveal the truth in death, this can be a problem. I did a reading during which an infidelity was revealed and an apology was conveyed to be passed on to another relative. I shared this with my client, who hadn't known about the affair, and she was understandably upset by the news.

My information was later confirmed by her father, giving my information validity, but at what price? Now my client has information about someone she loves that is, to say the very least, unflattering. The apology didn't give anyone closure and it changed the way a young woman remembers her grandfather.

Since that reading, I look at the information that I am provided to see if it serves a purpose other than to injure my client. The third party a message is being passed to is not my main concern; it's my client who comes first. This is the only circumstance where I intentionally withhold information, and again, it is rare. This episode caused me to create a code of ethics for myself. Sometimes it's as simple as common sense. Mediums must maintain high moral standards. After all, we've been given a great responsibility.

Clients inquiring about a spouse or lover aren't always happy with my predictions about their relationship, but I am always direct and I deliver all the information that I am provided. Of course, I wish everyone a happy romance. Unfortunately, I can't always tell my client that their relationship is forever. Keep in mind that gifted people can advise you in relationships, but we find more often than not that we are simply confirming something you already sensed yourself.

I have something to add for those who have discovered psychic abilities but aren't sure what to do with them: Just because you have a special gift does not mean you are obligated to turn it into your profession. Not all people with the gift function well advising others. It's absolutely okay to have another profession and direct your sixth sense toward expanding your success in that field. You also can choose to simply be a very spiritual person and funnel your gift into being a very well-balanced human being. Look outside the box for answers, because that's what the sixth sense is all about.

✦ Standards

I have learned to embrace my gift and know that it was given to me for a reason. I am well aware of how special my ability is, but I also know that responsibility comes with any gift. I have to use discretion and good judgment with it. For instance, if I am in a restaurant and see an elderly woman with her husband's spirit standing beside her, I can't just go up to her and share this with her.

I have a rule that unless the circumstances are right and I am asked for my input, I do not comment to strangers. I have to be careful about sharing information. I don't want to impinge on people's lives, especially with something that will impact them emotionally. I do this out of respect for people's individual beliefs.

I hold myself to a high standard, but I try to keep in mind that nobody is 100 percent all of the time. I am human and will not be consumed by impossible expectations. I am not a medium who shoots for what I call Kleenex points. I have seen people with my gift thrive on crying insincerely with their clients. Making people cry should not make you feel better about yourself. You can phrase a message in a less traumatic, more sensitive manner.

For example, if a son comes through and wants to convey to his mother that he loves her, that's no big surprise, so I would respond with the following: "Your son is expressing his love for you. He is acknowledging your mother-son connection." I have delivered the message in a kind way, sparing my client drama. That is nicer than saying, "Your son is expressing that nobody will ever love him the way you did and he's sorry that he caused you heartbreak. Life together would have been bliss."

Sometimes the medium has to interpret the feeling that is being conveyed, and the interpretation can play a part in how the message is delivered: dramatically, thoughtfully, angrily. One person might prefer a dramatic reading, whereas another might find that offensive. If you want a reading from a psychic, get a referral from someone you feel has good judgment.

You want to be able to connect with your

chosen medium, so spend a minute on the phone (if possible) and ask what you might expect from your reading. If you get a good feeling about the person, you have a better chance of your reading being everything you want it to be. Remember, don't give the medium personal information up front. Let them tell you specific details about yourself first. This will add impact and meaning to your reading.

After I've delivered the messages, I move through the reading, going back to special objects and memories from the deceased to authenticate their presence. Although it's important for the sitter to hear the loved one's message, it will be better received if she can reflect on the details later and remember the validating moments from her reading. I do not drag out and milk the sadness in readings. Tears are a common occurrence in a reading, but I prefer to bring out more happy elements.

My family is a different story; my usual rules may not apply. If I know that a family member is going to have a heart attack, I have to tell her, even if she's not open to what I do. My family is stuck with me and my gift. If I deliver the messages, I am fulfilling my obligation to them and to my calling.

Joe's deceased father came through to me one night. He was pacing back and forth beside our bed and the floorboards were creaking. (What a stereotypical haunt — creaking floorboards!) To my delight, Joe could hear his dad's efforts; for once I wasn't alone. We lay in bed for twenty minutes listening to Dad walk back and forth next to our bed. I just pulled the comforter over my head and tried to ignore him.

"What does he want?" Joe asked.

"I don't want to know. I'm tired."

"Allison, come on, ask him," Joe said.

"He says your brother needs to go to the doctor, but I'm not gonna tell him. He won't listen anyway."

The next night, as Joe and I got ready for bed, our alarm system went off. Joe checked it out and thought he had fixed the problem, even though we couldn't find the source of the activation. We went to sleep. At around 1:30 a.m. our alarm sounded again.

"Ask your guides what's wrong with the alarm," Joe said.

I asked and they answered: "The yellow wire is loose."

I repeated this to Joe and swore that as soon as I got up the alarm company was as good as there. I told Joe that his father was setting off the alarm, meaning he was alarmed about his son's health. The next morning a repairman from our alarm company came out. I asked him if the alarm system had a yellow wire, and if so, what it did. He said that there was a yellow wire and that it was connected to the face panel.

Of course, this meant nothing to me. The repairman went upstairs and grabbed a chair to stand on. The alarm box with the wiring in it was at the very top of my closet. He popped open the door and flashed his light on the wiring.

"Well, this is strange," he said. "The yellow wire is disconnected. When they hook these things up they secure the wiring." I saw it register on the repairman's face that the yellow wire I'd asked about was indeed loose. I wondered if he thought I did it on purpose to lure him there. I found it amusing to let his mind wander. Oh, well. The truth would probably have been harder for him to take anyway.

I called Joe and told him that it was in fact the yellow wire that was loose. Joe decided to call his brother at work the next morning. Joe was nervous. All we could hope for was that his brother would be somewhat open to the information and would go to the doctor for a checkup. Joe's brother works at a large engineering company and is very logical.

Joe called his brother's office. As soon as his brother picked up his business line, the company fire alarm was set off. Joe was stunned. His brother commented on how strange it was that his company's alarm had been triggered and that he'd have to call Joe back because he couldn't hear him over the alarm. Joe's dad had really gone all out to emphasize his message. Joe felt truly touched by this. He eventually passed the message on to his brother, but unfortunately my stubborn brother-in-law was not convinced to go to the doctor; he prefers to wait and see.

Chapter 11

Do You Really Want to Know?

A difficult aspect of being psychic is that sometimes people want to kill the messenger. Every now and then a client will be told something he does not want to hear and will turn on you. Sometimes it's easier to not believe a psychic than to face a difficult choice. I find that this occurs frequently with married people who want me to tell them what they want to hear.

"Do you really want to know everything?" I ask before I release sensitive information to clients. Frankly, some people don't, and I respect that. I am asking them to consider whether they want the impact of my information.

Often I learn I have pinpointed an area of weakness in their relationship that must be worked on to prevent a split. Sometimes the relationship is beyond saving because one or

169

both parties have already disconnected. There have been many occasions where an infidelity has taken place and I have shared the month that an affair will resume or end. I receive plenty of confirmation of my information, and since it's not always good news, I feel for my client.

I have decided that I will not answer certain questions about marriage. I won't answer if someone asks whether they made a mistake in marrying someone, or whether they really belong with someone else. I won't tell someone their marriage won't last. I am leery of upsetting someone's life, even if the information has been requested.

Most married people who have questions about their marriage already know where they stand with their spouses. I always tell clients to remember to live their lives as they wish and just use my information as an extra tool.

Part of advising people is learning to let go of the idea of making things right for everyone else. We mediums set boundaries for ourselves so we don't carry the weight of the world's problems on our shoulders. Help those you can, and respect people enough to let them find their own way in life. For those of you with a humanitarian save-the-world energy: I commend you, but please pick your fights carefully and don't let them destroy you.

✦ *Live!*

I was watching *Oprah* in July 2001 (yes, I watch *Oprah*!) when a man was featured who had nearly died in a plane crash twenty or so years earlier. He decided that if he survived he'd live life to the fullest and work to make a difference. He survived his close call and set out to really embrace life.

He was so inspiring! He made a list of one hundred things that he wanted to do before he died and so far he had accomplished around seventy of those things. I made a list of my own and wanted to share it with you and implore you to make your own list. As a matter of fact, you are reading one of my top ten goals on my to-do list: a book!

Near-death experiences seem to inspire people to live life to the fullest. Spare yourself the near-death experience — learn from others instead, and live! Life is like lightning, it's here and gone in an instant. Have a ball and share your beautiful gifts with others. Mentor a child, donate your time or money to a worthy cause like a hospice, or sign an organ donor card, it's free! Take it from me, you won't need your kidneys on the other side, and there is no more powerful gift than giving someone a new lease on life. Whatever you choose, pick something that moves you, something that reaches into the very core of who you are.

I always tap into the child who dwells within me, in order to not miss out on the little things in life. Remember when you were little and you wanted to save homeless animals and you couldn't understand why your parents were less than enthusiastic about taking in a pet that really needed you? You felt lucky to encounter a stray. Somehow you thought that you had been sent a special gift.

Growing up shouldn't mean giving up. Why do you think we stare at children in awe of their innocence and their unassuming discovery of life? We do this because part of us recognizes and misses that part of ourselves. Children are humanitarians naturally; most adults have to work at it. Either way, it's an inspiring characteristic.

Do you remember when you didn't understand why there were people in the world who were hungry? I remember my mom telling me that there were hungry people all over the world who would love to have the rest of my dinner. With childlike sincerity I suggested getting an envelope and sending them my dinner.

Today I have taken my childhood suggestion and applied it in an adult capacity. Every Thanksgiving and Christmas I write a check for holiday dinners at homeless shelters. I can't end world hunger, but I can make the holidays better for some people and let them know that they matter. Some people figure that if they can't end world hunger entirely, then they won't do anything at all, because it's easier to forget about a problem than to acknowledge that it exists and take action.

You must find the part of yourself that dared to dream that you could make a difference in people's lives. You can still create a positive ripple effect in the world. If you stop striving to connect with people you become isolated and self-absorbed. Growing up means that we gain the power to accomplish goals in the adult world, but somewhere along the way we start overlooking lost kittens and homeless people because it's easier to shut down than to feel for those in need.

I am not saying to make your house into an animal shelter. I am saying to look around and notice who needs help, and see what you might be able to do for them.

As for panhandlers, I am not comfortable giving money to people on the streets, but I will extend kindness in the form of fast food. On more than one occasion I've noticed a homeless person standing by the road asking for money near a drive-through. I like to pick up an extra hamburger or something and give it to them. I have received two different responses: the person is hungry and truly appreciates the food and the gesture, or the person is a con-artist playing on people's guilt.

Charity feeds the soul, but don't be a sucker. You don't have to save the world; just appreciate its complex beauty. There are many ways to make a difference, and they all start with reaching out. Sometimes I almost feel selfish being charitable because it makes me feel so euphoric. Those I've helped have given me a spiritual boost. Positive energy feeds on itself and comes back to you.

I wrote this chapter for people who feel empty inside, who are searching for a purpose or just want to feel good. It never hurts to take inventory of your soul. Are you fulfilled? Have you accomplished everything in life that you said you would? What do you stand for? Have you made a difference in someone's life? Look in the mirror and get to know who you grew up to be. Being a fulfilled person means that at the end of your physical life you have no real regrets.

✦ Another Side

I am sometimes asked if people really go to hell. On two similar occasions, I could bring through a spirit, but I couldn't get the spirit to engage in dialogue with the sitter. In one instance, I looked at my client and started describing some dark characteristics about her father. Besides his alcoholism and his frequent physical abuse of his family, he was also an adulterer and engaged in some deviant sexual behavior, which included seeing prostitutes.

When sharing such information, it's rather unsettling to feel the client's pain. She verified my information and was okay with it. I explained to her that her father had chosen to turn away from the light and that this in no way reflected on her. I think people can create their own hell and take it with them should they decide they don't want to part with their darker spiritual features. Good children can be born to sinister people, and vice versa. Don't spend your life paying for your family's choices. People don't look at you and see your family; they see only you. The client I spoke of whose father turned from the light is one of the most centered, kind, loving women I have ever met. She is an exceptional mother and is a friend to many lucky people.

A few times, in similar situations, the client has bolted up off the couch in less than fifteen minutes and said, "I just needed to know that he went where he belonged!" and left.

Psychics are not here to tell people how to live; we are just trying to give people insight into their future so they can make the most of their precious time on earth. I must admit it's hard to watch people fall back into life patterns that cost them their happiness. We can only advise and send people angels to guide them. The will of the human spirit can override all the guidance sent, so listen carefully to what you hear when you're sensing your truth.

Chapter 12

If You Never Die

To bring a relieved smile to a person's face after helping her gain closure with a deceased loved one means more to me than words can possibly say. I found myself on the other side of the table when my high school friend Domini died at age thirty-one.

I had known Domini since I was fourteen, when we met during my freshman year at North High. I remember the day we met at the bus stop in front of school. Domini was a gymnast; she looked feminine but was definitely able to handle herself if needed. She had the most captivating Julia Roberts smile. She was all teeth. She was friendly and approachable and we quickly struck up a conversation. After that we were fast friends.

Although Domini was vivacious and beautiful, she had a wounded, childlike spirit. Her childhood had been complicated and she longed to fit in and be loved. She was always the life of the party. She was diagnosed with malignant melanoma in July 2000 and died on April 2, 2001. It was hard watching my friend suffer.

Sometimes being psychic is difficult, because you know something awful is coming that you can't stop — you can only sit and watch your prediction unfold. For a long time, I'd had a strong feeling that Domini would die of cancer around the age of thirty. When I was about nineteen, I told her that I saw her life ending in about ten years and that cancer would be the culprit. I was not the only one who sensed her early demise.

In our teens, I had a moment with Domini that shall never escape me. She and I were best friends. We went to see the movie *Beaches*, starring Bette Midler. As the story on the screen unfolded, Domini turned toward me. We were at the part where Bette Midler's character was talking to her best friend (played by Barbara Hershey). Hershey was explaining to Midler that she had cancer and was going to die. Hershey wanted Midler to take care of her daughter after she passed away.

"Ali?" (Dom was the only one who ever called me Ali.) "If something happened to me and I died, would you do that for me?

Would you take care of my child and tell her all about me?"

I tried to lighten the mood by saying, "Well, not *all* about you."

But I saw that she was serious, so I reassured her. "Domini! Yes, of course I would."

"Do you promise?"

"Yes!"

Domini looked relieved. She knew that I am a stickler for keeping my word.

Our own lives paralleled the movie in many ways. Just a few years after this promise was made, Domini and her husband, Dominic, had a beautiful little daughter whom they named Marissa. But by my early twenties, I had lost contact with Dom. I was married, with my own family, and we went our separate ways.

I thought of her frequently and I wondered about her cute little redheaded girl, the baby whose diaper I had tried to change but invariably put on backwards. The toddler who received nothing but Happy Meals from me because I didn't know what to feed a small child. I had had no experience with children, but I tried, because I wanted to help Domini take care of her little girl. I wanted to know Marissa and for her to know me.

Six years went by, and then in 2000 I decided to find her. I ran a computer search and located her through Dominic, from whom she was divorced. The urgency that I felt about finding her was no coincidence. My guides were sending me to her for a reason. I told Domini that I was interning at the county attorney's office and she informed me that she was working down the street from me. For the next few months, Domini and I spent lots of time on the phone; it was as if like six years had never passed.

She had a new husband, and they'd had a baby girl that March. I offered to bring dinner over (she lived about an hour from me); I wanted to see her new baby. Joe and I loaded up the kids and went to spend the evening with Dom and her new family.

It was the first time I had seen Marissa since she was three years old. She was the same bright-eyed girl whom I remembered taking to McDonald's. The night seemed to pass much too quickly. We pored over scrapbooks full of old pictures and talked for hours; then it was time to go. The following week Dom's phone was disconnected and I did not hear from her for four long months.

In the summer of 2000 she was diagnosed with cancer and contacted me to share the news. She succumbed to her illness soon after. All those years ago, Dom and I had sat together watching a movie that was a glimpse into our future. We cried together and we laughed together, and later, when it was time, we said good-bye together. I believe that Domini knew as we watched that movie that her time on earth would be short. Domini had said so many times that she always knew that she would not grow old. She was right.

✦ *Until We Meet Again*

I don't like to say good-bye because it's too final. I like to say, "Till we meet again."

Domini spent several months fighting her cancer. I used my time with her wisely, making every moment count. Stacey, to whom I became close through Domini's illness, helped me fulfill some of Domini's last wishes. Closure is important for both the dying and the loved ones left behind. Don't be emotionally paralyzed by the unfortunate circumstances. If you're lucky enough to have this valuable time, consider yourself blessed. Ask what your loved one would like to do or see while she remains here. You have an opportunity that many people would give anything for.

Domini had always wanted a cute apartment, but cleaning and decorating weren't her strong suit. So Stacey and I cleaned her entire apartment while she was out. We added all-new, bright, cheerful home decorations. We burned candles and incense until we lost our sense of smell. Domini loved her apartment! She reveled in the floral aroma, and she delighted in each of the new little knickknacks that she found peppered throughout her apartment.

Domini had also stated that she really wanted a lobster for dinner. She hadn't always enjoyed the simple pleasures in life. Now she was taking the time to do just that. A lobster was easy enough to arrange. We took her out to dinner and talked about being sixteen years old.

When you're young you can't really fathom that your life will end. You don't think about what you'd want for a last meal or what you'd say to those you were about to leave behind. You have all the time in the world, and you live life fearlessly. You also don't realize that the choices you make in your teens can affect your entire life.

Over dinner, we talked with the wisdom of three women who had learned the hard way. At sixteen, we'd thought we knew it all, had done it all, and one day would have it all. Now we all agreed that being young is both a blessing and a curse. You have no cares and no worries, but you are lacking in good judgment when you need it the most. We laughed and cried about growing up and then we drove Dom back to her apartment to rest.

A few weeks before Domini's thirty-first birthday we had a just-like-old times party in her honor so that she could spend time with old friends. There is so much value in saying what needs to be said while people you love are still here. It goes a long way. My guides gave me the date of March 22, which both Stacey and I wrote on our calendars. They said that on that day something pivotal would happen in Domini's life. I knew that she wasn't going to pass on that day, so I prepared myself for whatever else might happen.

March 22 came and went. Stacey and I couldn't figure out what my guides had meant. The next day I received a call from Dominic, Domini's ex-husband. He said that Domini had gone into convulsions the night before and had been admitted to a hospice. Up until then, she had done everything in her power to stay out of a hospice. Even though she needed care, she chose to suffer at home. She knew in her heart that once she went in she wouldn't come out. Of course, her feeling was right.

At two o'clock on April 2, my guides told me to go see her. They even showed me the route that I would travel to see her. I had several readings booked, and as usual I was busy running around trying to take care of too many things at once. I looked at the clock at around 4:15 p.m. Every minute after that, my eyes were drawn back to the clock.

"What?" I said to my guides. "*Judge Judy* is half over; so what?" I went to an appointment and came home feeling sluggish. Everything seemed to be in slow motion. I walked in through the garage door. I looked up and saw my husband walking toward me. I shook my head and said, "Domini died, didn't she?"

Joe said, "Yes, she died at two-fifty this afternoon."

Sometimes I think I don't deserve my guides. I had so many things on my mind that I completely ignored their signs. They tried to get me to my friend to say good-bye one last time and I dismissed them. They tried to tell me she was passing, and I was too busy to receive their message.

The very next day after her death, I received some information from the other side that there was a ring in a white box that was intended for Domini's daughter Marissa. Domini hadn't been really clear about details after she was diagnosed with cancer and had not arranged to get the ring to Marissa, but it was very important to her. Domini was the eternal optimist and thought that she was going to beat the cancer. One way for her to keep from dying was to not tie up the loose ends.

This is a common practice among the dying. Many feel that death can't happen to them if they haven't said their good-byes. Unfortunately, death doesn't work that way.

I was told that the white box would be stuck under a mattress, or hidden by a mattress. I could see a mattress; a hand was lifting it at the corner and pointing. I had to try to interpret this vision. Clearly, Dominic needed to look under the mattress, so I called him to share this information.

I felt terrible calling Dominic, because he had taken care of Dom while she was dying and he had his own pain to deal with. I was there when they met thirteen years earlier. Although they didn't always see eye to eye, he never stopped loving her and he could not stop thinking of her, because they had so many similarities. Besides their names, they also shared the same birthday.

If you're wondering why Dominic cared for her and her new husband did not, it's because the second husband had stepped out of the picture as soon as Domini became sick. She apparently wasn't much fun for him anymore. A couple of months before she died, he filed for divorce. Fortunately for him, it hadn't yet gone through, so he could still receive benefits from her death. I have one word for him: karma.

Dominic called later that day. He had found the box with the ring in it, stuck between a mattress and a nightstand. I said, "Is the box white? Because if it isn't in a white box, I won't feel confirmation." (I can be a little demanding of my gift. Plus, my dear friend had passed away and I wanted to be absolutely sure that I was receiving her loud and clear).

"Yes, Allison, it's white, just like you said."

Dominic's spirits seemed to lift once he knew Domini was communicating with us. She was sending a sign to those she loved that she was all right. More important, she was handing her ring over to her little girl Marissa, with love from the other side.

Most people would expect a medium to

handle a friend's death much more gracefully than would an average person. But after Domini died, I was like any grieving person. I felt as if I had been caught with my guard down. I have always seen the dearly departed attending their own funerals and felt comforted by that. At Domini's funeral I felt no such comfort.

As I watched her children play in the cemetery, unaware of the enormity of the occasion, I felt as though I'd been punched in the chest. The children seemed to run in slow motion, and their laughter was haunting. As I stood next to Domini's casket I could feel the physical weight of her body inside the casket along with her cancer. I felt sick and I tried to remember her before the cancer found its way through her body.

I think of Domini all the time. I recall the feeling of her cancer and remember the last time we sat together before she died. I didn't want to leave her then because I knew that I would never see her alive again. Cancer had reduced her to a shadow of her former physical self. As I held her, I feared I would break her because she was so fragile. Saying good-bye when you know it's for the last time is like no other sadness you will ever experience.

I know that Domini isn't in pain any longer; she's restored and vivacious again. Still, although I know that she is in a better place, I feel that her energy, as I knew it, has been removed from my world.

I also feel guilty. Domini had just had a baby, a year before she died. I saw her right after the baby was born, and I told her that something was wrong with her physically. She insisted that it was because she had just had a baby. I told her it wasn't from having a baby. I persisted and made her promise to see a doctor. She reluctantly promised me at first, but then she said that she'd just seen a doctor, who said that she was fine.

This is where I find myself in a difficulty. I know that I couldn't have changed the outcome of Dom's life, but part of me feels that because I've done it for other people, I should have been able to intervene for her. But it was not to be. Domini had experienced a great deal of pain while she was pregnant, but her doctors thought it was because of her pregnancy. By the time she was diagnosed it was too late: her cancer was inoperable. I, too, must learn the lesson that you cannot blame yourself when you lose someone you love. Sometimes it's out of our hands.

Domini's two youngest children will not

have a clear memory of her, although I have no doubt they will receive regular visits from their mother. She would have it no other way.

I try to remember that there is a reason for everything, but I am human and feel great sadness when someone's life experiences are limited. I've also learned that it's all right to mourn. Crying and asking why is a healthy way of working through your grief. I encourage people to talk to their loved ones on the other side. They will not only listen to you; they will answer you, one way or another.

When someone has passed prematurely, my ability to bring some sort of comfort is particularly important to me, because the wound is so raw for those left behind. Loved ones who remain to pick up the pieces have many unanswered questions. One of the biggest is "Why did you leave me?"

The answer can be an antidote for the pain, or it can add to the sense of loss. There is solace in knowing that we stay connected even beyond death and that there are reasons for every ending and beginning. Please know that your loved one simply got to go first. They will greet you when it's your turn and it will be like no other family reunion you've ever experienced.

Our loved ones who cross over still go through life with us. They act as added energy when you need it. When you need strength, you might call out to your grandfather on the other side for strength and guidance. When you need patience, you might ask your mother to calm you. I know that when I get too serious, Domini is the burst of fun energy that tells me to lighten up. Allow your loved ones to be a part of you and provide inspiration in your life.

I once had the opportunity to do a reading for a nice gentleman and his wife. I asked him whether he had a brother on the other side who died as a child.

He said no.

"That's strange," I said, "because the energy is a brother energy."

"Oh," he said, "I had a nephew who died when he was twelve. We were very close in age; we were like brothers. We grew up together. His name was Martin."

"Did he wear leg braces?"

"Yes, he did," Martin's uncle said.

Martin expressed concern over his parents. He worried that his death drove a wedge between them, and he went into detail about how they still grieve for him. He wanted closure for them. I explained to Martin that his parents would not be open to this experience. Martin kept giving me the names Robert and Bobby. I turned to Martin's uncle and asked, "Who are Robert and Bobby to Martin? Martin's being persistent."

"Martin isn't my nephew's first name. His first name is Robert, and his middle name is Martin. Bobby is Martin's father's name."

Martin was terribly concerned about his father's well-being and had many nostalgic memories to share with his uncle. His uncle wanted to share Martin's messages with Martin's father. He hoped that Bobby would be willing to listen. Some people are not ready to hear messages from the other side and some people are not ready to give messages from the other side. It's a shame, because when those on both sides are willing to take part in a meeting, there is a great opportunity for healing and closure. It's healthy to remain open to life's possibilities.

✦ Pets: Do They Live On?

Recently I had a personal dilemma. My old cat, Sinbad, was sick and didn't look well. I like to think of myself as a compassionate person and I have always tried to do the right thing in life. Sinbad was ill and physically deteriorating. But I had known him for eleven years! My mom had found him ripped apart by coyotes and had nursed him back to health. He was a young yet full-grown cat then, and we weren't quite sure how old he was — probably somewhere between thirteen and sixteen.

Sinbad had survived an attack by coyotes. Why should I cause his demise? I could feel that Sinbad was suffering, but I didn't want to take away his remaining days. I knew that if I took him to the vet I wouldn't walk out with him in my arms. He loved to lounge in the grass in our front yard and he enjoyed basking in the sunshine. I deal with the other side on a daily basis and know it to be a kind and beautiful place, but I loved my cat and wasn't ready to lose him. What would he want me to do?

I feared making the wrong decision. He was a family member. It was a Friday night and I decided to talk to my guides. I couldn't make a decision like this without help. Some people don't see the significance of pets, but I do. Sinbad was important. I asked my guides what I should do and I received some feedback, but nothing earth-shattering. I became frustrated and said to my guides, "You make it possible for me to give other people clear answers to their problems. I can deliver messages and give peace of mind to others, so why not to myself? I need something special, something magical."

There's nothing like a young medium throwing a temper tantrum at the other side. After hours of inner reflection I fell asleep, tossing and turning. That night I was given exactly what I had asked for. It came in the form of an amazing dream. (Anyone who knows me knows that I rarely dream at all.) At the time I was not aware that it was a dream because it seemed so real:

My friend Domini was alive and we were in her apartment. I was looking at my scrapbooks and I noticed that everything was cleaner than usual in Domini's apartment. She walked around the corner, coming toward me. She looked younger than I was, even though I knew her to be two years older. I had always been the baby in our group of friends. Domini had her hair pulled back into a fluffy blond ponytail. Her childlike blue eyes contained sparks of gold light and she looked flawless. In came Dominic. He walked past her, and they brushed shoulders but neither one flinched. Dominic walked through the apartment and into another room, closing the door.

Meanwhile, Domini was in the living room playing with a baby, but I wasn't sure whose. I was tired and decided to go home, so I collected my scrapbooks as I headed for the door. Domini said, "Ali! Wait!" She gestured for me to come back. I walked over to her and set my books down on the table. Domini began thumbing through the pages of my books and every now and then she would look at me and smile contently. I told her I had to go and walked out the door, but now instead of being in the hallway, I was in the lobby of a vet's office. I turned around to ask Domini what was going on. She smiled and gently nodded her head toward me.

I snapped out of my sleep and sat up in bed. My first reaction was to call Domini and tell her I'd had a dream about her, but then I remembered that she had died three months earlier. I had asked my guides for an incredible sign. The one that I was given had many special meanings to me. Out of the many personally significant events in my dream, two messages really stood out. First, Domini was letting me know that she still functions around Dominic and is still with him. Before she died, Domini told me that she was certain she would be able to contact me from the other side. She also said it comforted her to know she would be able to reach out to those she loved.

By showing me the vet's office, Domini was making me feel that Sinbad would be all right, that taking him to the vet was the compassionate thing to do for him. I knew Domini was telling me that she would take care of him. Shortly after my dream, we took Sinbad to the vet to be put down. The vet told us that he had intestinal cancer and that there was nothing they could do for him. We loved him enough to let him go. Although I'd known that Sinbad was going to pass away that year, it didn't hurt any less just because I knew ahead of time.

Ironically, our new cat came from Domini. As her illness had progressed, she could no longer care for some kittens she had, so I had brought one home to my kids. We named our kitten Caesar. We still have him, and my family treats him like a little king. He is a breath of fresh air. I love it that Caesar is full of life, as Domini was. The only thing about him I don't like is his tendency to pounce on my head in the middle of the night and ruffle my hair with his paws. This I cannot get used to. But it seems right that we have one of Domini's cats. I have no doubt that she is caring for

Sinbad on the other side, even though he might be a little mellow for Domini's high-energy personality.

Pets have been significant factors in many readings. They are part of our lives and many people consider theirs to be family members. Although I knew that cats and dogs crossed over, I wasn't aware that birds could come through from the other side until I encountered one very small family member during a reading.

The client was a very energetic, comical woman who had recently lost someone, but she didn't say whom. I sat with her for a minute and immediately saw a clear picture of a woman with dyed hair wearing a Hawaiian muumuu and lei. I had a hard time wiping the smile off my face, because the woman was extremely amusing. I told my client that the woman was a mother figure and I asked whether she either was going to Hawaii or had come from there.

My client gasped. "We were going to Hawaii together, and my mother-in-law died before our trip." Obviously, my client was moved by her mother-in-law's acknowledgment of the much anticipated trip.

Then I saw something that I had not seen before. A bird was perched on the mother-in-law's finger. She seemed quite fond of it,

196

so I asked, "Did she have a bird? Because she's showing me one on her finger."

"Yes," she replied. "She had two birds, Ike and Tina. Tina died around the time my mother-in-law passed."

I had never before witnessed a pet other than a cat, dog or horse, but now I had seen a bird. This was just further confirmation for my client, which truly connected her with her mother-in-law on the other side.

Chapter 13

Once in a Lifetime

When I approached Diane about including her reading in my book, she said she'd be honored. But actually I am the one who is honored, to have met such a resilient, charming woman. Diane hopes that her story will provide comfort to others who face similar challenges. This chapter might also give insight to those of you who have never had a reading. Diane's story will give you an idea of what can occur when one is visiting with the other side.

Diane was a light-eyed, free-spirited young woman who easily made friends. Jim was a vibrant, loving, good-looking young guy. They met in high school in 1968. She was fifteen and he was seventeen. They parted ways when Jim went into the service, but they were reunited a few years later and married within a month. They were happy together and embraced their new family.

In the 1970s, five years and two months

into their wedded bliss, their time together was cut short.

Fast forward to 2001, when I met her. Diane showed up for a group session hoping to hear from someone special on the other side. I stepped forward and hugged her; we then took our seats to begin the session. When Diane's turn came, she asked if I saw anyone with her. I told her I saw a man who looked to be from the early 1970s, with a mustache but no beard. He was saying something about his hair being somehow significant to him. It was shorter on the sides than in the back. He was wearing tight jeans and had a cute butt. He was highly attractive, with a stunning smile. He was tall, thin, and broad-shouldered, and he was showing me an acoustic guitar.

Diane said, "That's my husband, Jim. He had a mustache and no beard because he wasn't able to grow a beard." Diane seemed amused by that.

I said, "He died of head trauma at the hands of another person." Diane confirmed this and added that Jim had died in the 1970s.

"He keeps showing me a smoke-filled room, like a bar." Diane shared that Jim had indeed met his killers in a bar.

"He's telling me that there was a woman

involved in his murder. He says he didn't die right away. He also says that the people responsible were convicted of a lesser charge but that they are still paying for what they did to him." Diane said that indeed there was a woman involved in Jim's murder, the people responsible were convicted of a lesser charge, and Jim had not died right away.

Jim then told me to tell Diane that he was sorry. Diane said she understood everything and not to be sorry. I told her that Jim said he always knew she was a smart woman, and that Jim was sharing with me that he had known in advance it was his time to go. Diane responded that Jim had always said he thought he would die before thirty, and that he was twenty-six when he passed. Often people have a sense of when their life will draw to a close.

While being interviewed for this book, Diane divulged the events leading up to Jim's death. I am sharing the details so that young people realize that we have to be careful about whom we trust. People can change their tune in an instant. I hope that Jim's story can make people more aware of their personal safety.

Diane was glad to share her story because it helps to talk about what happened to her husband. There are always loved ones left in the aftermath of such selfish and violent acts like the one causing Jim's death. The survivors need closure and remembrance of those they've lost.

This is my way of memorializing Jim for the good person he was. Jim is now gone, and one day his killers will have to answer for what they've done. Although I believe in a loving God, I also believe in a just God. The acts of violent criminals are always remembered in the end.

The people who killed Jim were slight acquaintances, but he trusted them because it was in his character to trust. People who would never hurt others usually assume that everyone values human life in the same way. Unfortunately, they don't.

Jim got into a car with a woman and two men he had met that night for the first time at the bar; they went to see if a mutual acquaintance was home, but he wasn't. They were headed back to the bar when a dispute erupted between the passengers. The driver pulled the car over one block from the bar, slamming on his brakes so hard that the noise roused a married couple in a nearby house from their sleep. The witnesses saw Jim and the driver exit the vehicle. The driver karate-kicked Jim in the head and knocked him to the ground. The female then joined in the assault by kicking Jim in the head repeatedly with her platform shoes.

A second male attacker exited the vehicle and also kicked Jim. He then grabbed the fender of the vehicle for leverage while jumping on Jim's already injured head. The original male attacker then pulled the second male off Jim and they took off in their car. One of the neighbors who witnessed the attack ran to Jim's aid and held him while waiting for the paramedics to come. Jim's only words to the woman were "Where is my wife?"

Jim regained consciousness in the hospital, where he identified his attackers (they were arrested.) Jim also told Diane to call her mother so that he could talk to her. Jim was very close to Diane's mother and thought of her as his own mom. He called her up and weakly said, "Mom, I'm coming home." Whatever he meant by that, he died within two weeks. Diane was certain that Jim knew he wasn't going to make it.

While I was interviewing Diane for my book, she shared with me that three days before we met, Jim had made himself known to her through a dream. Sometimes it's easier for spirits to reach us in our dreams because our defenses are down when we sleep.

In our group session, I said to Diane that Jim had come to her before in a dream; this served as validation for her. In her dream Jim put his arms around Diane and held her, saying "I've waited a long time for this."

To clarify Diane's interpretation of this statement, I'll preface it with a brief explanation. Prior to our reading, Diane had contacted a show featuring a medium; she wanted to attend, hoping for closure on her husband's death. Her kids had checked the phone messages and apparently had lost the call-back information left by the show. Diane was disappointed at missing the opportunity. A coworker had told her about my group sessions; the rest is history.

Diane felt that Jim had repeatedly tried to bring her to a third party (a medium) to receive confirmation of his presence. She said she was certain that visiting a medium was what she was supposed to do. She understood Jim's statement to mean that he'd been waiting a long time for her to receive validation and closure.

During Diane's reading, I had given her a message from Jim. She did not share with me what it meant until much later, when interviewed for this book. I had told her that Jim said there was a dark-haired man whom he didn't trust. Jim said to tell her, "He hasn't changed, so don't be fooled."

Diane said this was what convinced her beyond a doubt that Jim had come through to her. She said that her husband was a nice guy who trusted absolutely everybody, with the exception of one relative; Jim was so leery of this man that he wasn't permitted in their home.

This relative came to see him in the hospital after the assault. As soon as he left the hospital room, Jim grabbed Diane's collar, pulled Diane down to him and whispered in her ear, "Don't trust him, he hasn't changed, so don't be fooled." Jim had given me the words that meant the world to Diane. There were only three people who knew of this episode: Jim, Diane, and her mother. Diane had never shared the story with anyone else until now.

Jim was making it clear as he came through that it was important to him to acknowledge a daughter, so I asked Diane whether he had one. She hesitated and then said that yes, he had a stepdaughter. Jim was ruffled by this answer and conveyed to me that he considered her *his* daughter. I shared this with Diane, and she smiled. She said Jim used to get mad when people called Angie his stepdaughter and he'd always correct them. Even in death, his feelings hadn't changed.

I told Diane to tell Angie that Jim said he plays with his grandchildren. (Diane shared this with Angie after the reading, and Angie said she knew it. She said her little ones always seem amused by something that seemingly isn't there.) Diane went on to tell me that she has six grandchildren and was quickly corrected by Jim, who said, "Not you — we have six grandchildren."

Jim's love for his daughter, Angie, was deep. When he was alive he told Diane that he wouldn't have been capable of fathering a child as beautiful as Angie, so someone else had to bring her into the world for him to raise. Angie was one year old when Jim came into her life.

I was able to learn a great deal from Jim's spirit. He had shown me an acoustic guitar at the beginning of our reading. Jim's father played acoustic guitar and Jim used to sit with him while he recorded music. Jim's son also played the guitar as a teenager, so the guitar could have symbolized a couple of things, showing the connection between grandfather, son, and grandson. It was also nice to see that Jim and his father were together on the other side.

It's especially difficult for young people when they lose someone. We all would like to think that a visiting spirit would soothe the living, but often this is not the case. When a living person is mourning the loss of a deceased loved one, the spirit tends to want to be close for support.

Sometimes this can be a catch-22. When a spirit's energy is around us, we can feel it. We long for those we miss instead of realizing they're actually in our presence, spending time with us, feeling our pain. Sensing all the sadness, the spirit will then try harder to bring energy through to console us, which can cause all sorts of reactions in the survivor: pictures flashing through the mind, hearing a song play in the head, feeling a cold draft, feeling as though one is being touched.

Sometimes this can make the living person long for the dearly departed even more and cause even greater heartache. I don't believe spirits realize that their presence is aggravating the pain caused by their loss. The same effect can be felt when a spirit wants to be around loved ones, and the living think that they have thought of the deceased out of the blue.

In this situation a normal reaction is "I

haven't thought of that person in a while. I wonder what triggered that memory." In reality, the visiting energy has caused us to retrieve feelings and memories that surround their being. If we are open to the thought that our loved ones remain with us after death, we can understand the relationship that we have with them after they die physically.

If you can't wrap your mind around this thought, at least know that you and those you love who have crossed over will be together again when your time comes and you are invited over to the other side. Don't be in a hurry for your reunion. We are here to learn and enjoy life, and for each one of us, our day will come.

Jim was the only spirit I brought through for Diane that day; he was the visitor she had hoped for. He is by far one of my favorite people on the other side. He has the heart of Santa Claus, the trust of a child, and the humor of a friend who is always trying to cheer you up when you're down. I can't do him justice through my description — some people are beyond words. When Jim started pulling his energy back, the last thing he said to Diane was, "We will always be together, and when the day comes that you cross over to the other side I will be there to greet you."

Jim showed me his hand lovingly extended to take Diane's, as though helping her out of one life and into another (but not anytime soon). Diane expressed closure and satisfaction. She said that she was entirely engulfed by a calm, peaceful, good feeling after her reading. Diane is one of the reasons I continue to do what I do.

Chapter 14

Baby Boy

When Domini found out that she was dying, she reached out to her old friends, one of whom was Stacey. I've known Stacey for thirteen years, through my association with Domini. We were frequently around each other in our teenage years, but we hadn't become close friends.

Domini was over at Stacey's house getting ready to come over for a party I was throwing in her honor so that Dom could be around the old gang one last time before she passed. Domini put us in an awkward situation when she handed the phone to Stacey and forced us into a conversation. It turned out that Stacey and I live only a couple of miles apart and we have the same sarcastic sense of humor. Strangely enough, Stacey and I clicked immediately and made a play date for our kids for the following week.

Stacey was pregnant with her second

child, whom she had already decided to name Trevor, and like any excited mom she was eager to show off her son's ultrasound pictures. She handed them to me and I admired the small form.

"Domini told me what you do. Is there anything wrong with him?" Stacey asked.

I hesitated, then ran my hand over the ultrasound; my hand stopped around his lower abdominal area. "He's perfect up until here," I said, pointing to his kidneys.

Stacey said, "Oh yeah, the doctor said one kidney is bigger than the other, but they said that's normal for boys, and it'll correct itself in the womb."

I wasn't sure whether I should reply truthfully and upset a pregnant woman I was hoping to become friends with, or lie and let Stacey find out later in her pregnancy.

But she prodded me: "You can tell me."

"Well, he has a serious problem with his kidneys, but it's correctable. They have a medical procedure they can do in utero."

Stacey said, "You mean they'll have to go into me? They said they wouldn't do anything before he was born, and they said it'll correct itself in utero."

Stacey was clearly troubled by this information, and understandably so. She asked what else I saw. I told her that after Trevor was born they would have to perform another procedure, a fairly common one, and that he'd be fine.

Stacey felt enough anxiety to go in for an early checkup for Trevor, but she truly felt that everything would be fine and that the doctor would tell her that the kidney had already corrected itself. Unfortunately, that was not the case. The nurse called in Stacey's doctor to take a closer look at her condition. Stacey was informed that the baby's kidneys were distended and so was his bladder. Tests confirmed that he might be going through renal failure, and his amniotic fluid was low. She was referred to a specialist and told the outlook wasn't good.

Stacey called me in tears. "You were right, there's a problem."

This was one of those occasions when I would have been overjoyed to be wrong.

The doctor kept saying, "I'm sorry, Stacey." Stacey asked him if there was any chance Trevor could make it. The doctor said, "Let me talk to my colleague and get back to you."

The doctors wanted to retest the fluid, and this time the results were even worse. Stacey called me for consolation, but all I could say was "He will be fine, Stacey. This is one of the most difficult experiences that you will ever endure in your lifetime, but I can tell you that Trevor will be born, and he will be fine."

I was afraid that I appeared to be a condescending, callous know-it-all, but I knew what I told her would turn out to be right.

I went on to tell her about her grandfather on the other side, who was "tinkering" (a term she said he used) with his own form of intervention for Trevor. Her grandfather came through with details, one of which was that nobody was winding his cuckoo clock and he wanted Stacey to do so. I told her it was the clock that was brown with big black maple leaves on it. Stacey said she knew exactly which one I was talking about. This was important information to have shared, because it validated something personal between Stacey and her grandfather.

He also wanted her to know that she wasn't alone and that he was doing what he could from the other side. I sat on the phone with her and listened to her sob uncontrollably, feeling powerless to do anything but be there for her.

Within a week, Stacey's new specialist, Dr. Foley, suggested a new procedure that was being used in England. It involved going into the unborn baby's abdomen and inserting a shunt into his bladder that would allow urine to pass through and produce the amniotic fluid necessary to keep him alive long enough to be born. Surgery was scheduled for the day before Thanksgiving, and Stacey was excited.

Everything went well until the shunt broke. Dr. Foley had only seen this happen once before and there was no backup shunt, so the procedure was unsuccessful. When Stacey had given up on ever seeing her baby alive, the compassionate Dr. Foley looked at her and said, "Let me be your hope."

Stacey sure wasn't feeling thankful that year. She called me upset, worried that Trevor wouldn't even make it through the weekend. His amniotic fluid was dangerously low and he would be unable to breathe if he ran out. I tried to console her.

"He's just fine. He's a mellow baby, but he's tough, too."

Stacey wanted to believe me, but how could she feel optimistic now? On Monday, Stacey's doctor conducted another ultrasound. Stacey was expecting to hear that Trevor's condition was the same, or perhaps even that he had not survived. She was not expecting what happened next. The doctor excitedly pointed out the increase in amniotic fluid; it was now at a normal level. He had only ever seen this happen once before and that case is in the books. Trevor was a miracle. Still, Stacey would not allow herself to get her hopes up.

I bonded with Trevor while he was in utero. I knew how he was feeling, what he'd look like, what his temperament was, and if he could be willed here I was going to do it. I did a lot of soul-searching and asked my guides many questions about life and what really matters. All along they assured me this baby was going to be here and that there were forces from the other side who were helping him.

On February 18, 2001, my godson Trevor Jon (after Stacey's grandfather) Michael (after Dr. Michael Foley, whom Stacey will forever love for saving her baby) was born. I was there when he came into the world. I had to be there to know he was okay the second he was born. The little brute weighed almost eight pounds, and he was four weeks early!

I had told Stacey before Trevor was born that he'd have light eyes like her side of the family, not dark brown like her husband and daughter. He would also have his father's wavy hair. He would be built like a linebacker and be the most tranquil, happy baby she'd ever seen. He looks and acts exactly as I saw him before he was born. I knew him long before we were formally introduced.

Trevor did have to have kidney surgery right after he was born. Stacey said she wasn't upset about this since I had already told her about it four months earlier. Knowing this made me sure that I had done the right thing in telling Stacey about Trevor's future medical procedures.

I also told Stacey that Trevor would be taken off a particular medication at six months, which he was. She asked me about a surgery that Trevor was supposed to have after his first year, and I shared that between six and nine months of age he'd need this surgery, but he'd be fine. The doctors insisted that Trevor would need to be older than the time frame I'd given.

Well, my resilient little man had the surgery at nine months and the doctors said that it was lucky they'd performed it early. It turned out that complications would have occurred had his condition not been addressed at that time.

Let me make it clear that Trevor was being taken care of by forces other than me. He was already covered. It was Stacey I was taking care of, through my predictions. Now

Stacey uses her own intuition regularly and is persistent when she pursues answers from Trevor's doctors. Her ability to trust her own instincts has been a benefit to her son and his future. Intuition is so important when it comes to health issues. If you're not satisfied with your doctor's advice, get a second opinion. Your doctor's feelings won't be hurt.

Trevor has already taught me several valuable lessons. One is the incredible power of faith. Remember to hold yours tight. Another is that intervention from the other side is one way that our love continues even after we've crossed over. Never underestimate undying love. I also realized how much a crisis either brings people together or tears them apart. Stacey is my closest friend and we will always look back on her pregnancy with Trevor and know that we were brought together at that time for a reason.

I once did a reading for a young woman who had lost her husband and could not recover from the pain of losing him. I spent most of the session giving her details about him and messages from him. My client asked about having children; she had been told that she most likely could not. I told her that there was indeed scarring but that she was capable of getting pregnant and would have a child within two years. I am happy to report that a year later she gave birth to twin daughters.

Another meaningful medical moment happened to the person closest to me. One morning I was sitting at the breakfast table when Joe's deceased grandfather came through and said that Joe needed to go to the doctor and have his heart checked, and that he would understand, because heart trouble runs in the family. I told Joe, who knows that when I give a message he should take it seriously.

He made an appointment with his doctor, who put him through a series of tests, including some blood work. The results showed that he had extremely high triglycerides and high cholesterol. I had told him before that I was concerned about him passing at around age forty. Indeed, the doctor said he was lucky to have caught these conditions when he did, or Joe would have had a heart attack by forty. Strangely, my husband is not overweight and neither of his parents has died of a heart condition. I thank God for my gift for many reasons, but I am especially grateful that my husband will be here to watch our little girls grow up.

There have been many occasions where I've told people to have their chest X-rayed or have some other medical exam, and it turned out they had a rare form of tuberculosis or were in an early stage of breast cancer. I see this as being given a window to intervene for those who need the guidance of the other side.

Occasionally I run across a case where there is to be no intervention. I have had a really hard time coming to terms with that. Once you get used to making a positive difference in others' lives, it's hard to accept that you cannot help all people. Sometimes injury or premature death is meant to happen in someone's life plan. Why? Because without some misfortune we wouldn't be forced to acknowledge how precious life is. What is even more amazing is that sometimes there is intervention from the other side and that prayers can be answered.

Chapter 15

Loving a Medium

by Allison's husband, Joe

Allison asked if I would like to add anything to her book. I was not expecting that. This is her project. I am supposed to be the nonpsychic in the family. I'm an aerospace engineer, for God's sake! I've never seen a ghost. I heard one once, but I have never seen one. In any case, I was honored and I accepted her offer. Then I was on my own.

Where should I start? Do I talk about how we met? Or about when I discovered my wife is a psychic medium? About our daily routine? Who usually wins our arguments? Whether she constantly reads my mind? These are questions I get all the time, and I think they are all worth touching upon. The things I find most interesting are the things that Allison would not tell you herself.

When I first saw Allison, it was as if a

light shone down on her from above. She was surrounded by potential suitors, but was obviously not interested in any of them. Despite a completely bungled introduction, we managed to connect on some level. I did not see her again for several weeks, but then we began to date and within a year we were engaged. At this point I did not know that she was a psychic medium, even though she always seemed to know what I was thinking. Of course, this did not surprise me at the time because most women tend to know what men think.

One of the first undeniable times she revealed a glimpse of her full abilities was when I took her on a trip to San Francisco to ask for her hand in marriage. While on the trip we stopped at the Ripley's Believe It or Not Museum.

While there, we played a game in which each of two people tries to guess what the other is thinking. The physical setup consists of a panel that keeps the two people from seeing each other. On either side of the panel there are identical sets of buttons, each corresponding to a shape, such as a circle, star, or square. One person chooses a button and presses it. Then the other person tries to press the matching button without being able to see the opponent.

There is a set of lights to indicate if the guess was correct and an awful noise to indicate if it was not.

Five times in a row, Allison correctly chose the buttons I had pushed. I was confused. There was only a 1 in 3,125 chance of that happening. I thought the machine was broken, so I checked. It was not broken. I made her repeat the buttons in the order in which she pressed them. She was right on. I should have fallen to my knees and proposed right then!

She still did not reveal to me her psychic ability. It was not enough that she always knew people's motives or that she could always guess the endings to stories. I knew that she was an excellent driver, as if she was always able to see the hole in traffic before it opened up. These things alone were too subtle to notice, and besides, I was in love, so everything she did seemed special.

Shortly before I became fully aware of her ability, an odd thing happened. One afternoon when we were next in line at an automatic car wash, she looked at the car in front of us and started laughing.

"Wouldn't it be funny if the car in front of us was covered in suds and the machine broke and didn't rinse it off?"

Strangely, that was just what happened.

The guy in front of us waited a minute, then got out of his car and looked around with the funniest expression on his face. He then drove off, I presume to complain to the management.

At the time, I was not sure whether Allison saw the future or was actually able to make things happen. But the extent of her gift would soon be revealed, and many of my questions would be answered, only to raise more questions.

One day, Allison's senses were turned up higher than usual. She could see all sorts of spirits around the house, and was a little uneasy about it. I asked her what was bothering her.

"Like you don't know," she snapped. Well, of course I didn't know. I could not see them. I asked her repeatedly, and finally she told me what she was seeing. After she realized that, even though I could not see them, I would not condemn her for her ability, messages came flooding out from my relatives who had passed.

My father was one of the first to come though. He had passed away two and a half months before I met Allison. I missed him and for a long time I wished that he and Allison could have met. She told me about the drawing table where I would build model airplanes as a boy while my father watched over my shoulder. She detailed the models I made and hung over my bed, and she described my childhood room. She knew things that she could not have known about except psychically. It turned out to be a wonderful way to introduce me to her abilities. I think that she was also relieved to be able to open up to me completely.

Daily life with Allison is not as difficult as you might expect. But it is different. Some people like the expression "It is easier to beg forgiveness than ask permission." Well, this approach does not work with Allison. She feels betrayed, because she knows right away that you lied to her. I learned early in our marriage to be up front about everything. The small disagreements are quickly forgotten when addressed before the fact.

Allison has what she calls vivid recall. She can remember everything. Many husbands claim that their wives have this ability, and maybe it is true. But Allison remembers the clothes, the people, the food, the gifts, and the atmosphere of every birthday, holiday, and anniversary that we have had over the last decade.

I never have to worry about losing her in the mall or at an amusement park. She always seems to know right where I am.

Sometimes I forget when I am out with other people that they will not be able to find me so easily.

I feel that any two people who are truly in love are also in tune with each other; we give new meaning to the saying "Are you thinking what I'm thinking?" Most married couples feel a strong connection. Imagine that feeling turned up with a 20 dB gain (engineer talk for 100 times more powerful).

Allison often uses this unseen connection to improve our lives. She often calls on the telephone when I think of her. Other times she will remind me to take an extra dollar on a short trip to the store. I will not understand why until I get to the store and the bank machine is out of order. Now I have gotten used to these things.

We have spent many nights together with her relaying messages to me from the dead. Mostly these messages are from relatives, but some are from famous people. The spirits usually come through with something to verify their authenticity. For instance, my grandfather said he specifically missed Boston clam chowder. We called my mother, who confirmed that Boston clam chowder was one of his absolute favorites.

Another time, I inquired about Albert

Einstein and she came through with the cross streets of the university he attended in Germany. I've also received messages pertaining to future events in my life, some of which I am waiting to confirm.

Throughout much of this book there are examples of the fantastic things that Allison does. This is only one part of her. She is also a wife, a mother, and a friend. Like almost everyone, Allison is tired after a hard day's work. She likes to unwind by watching mindless television, like game shows and sitcoms. But sometimes she turns on a forensic science show in which they are extracting a bug's larva from the nose of a decomposed corpse to build a case against the perpetrator. I ask her if this is really relaxing, but she does not answer because she is so entranced.

I am scientific at heart and I want an explanation for her ability. I have been studying her habits and conducting small tests of my own. I hope that one day I will be able to offer an explanation of how she does it. However, I don't think that the question "Why her?" will be fully answered in this lifetime.

Chapter 16

Science and the Other Side

 *Lab Rat*

I was watching *Dateline* in the winter of 2001 when I saw a story on Dr. Gary Schwartz and John Edward. John Edward's psychic ability was being put to the test and Dr. Schwartz was talking about his research on the survival of human energy after death. My guides told me that I was to be a part of Dr. Schwartz's research and that I had to contact him. My guides never steer me wrong, but I knew nothing about being a research medium. I liked the idea of science being fused with the other side, but could I be effective there?

Dr. Schwartz is the director of the Human Energy Systems Laboratory at the University of Arizona in Tucson. He is known worldwide for his academic research on life after death. It took about a month to get in to meet with this busy man. If you're a psychic looking for confirmation from Gary that you're significant, forget it. Gary looks at you to study you, not to praise you. I like that about him. He's a scientist, not a groupie. I now sarcastically refer to myself as Gary's lab rat.

I grew increasingly excited about the meeting. I was going to get some third-party, objective validation from science. I wasn't looking for a pat on the back, just a test to gauge my ability. I was willing to be wrong or even to fail a test. I just had to know, for myself, whether I could measure up to my own expectations. I wanted feedback from an academic familiar with the spiritual field.

After a month of waiting, the day finally came for me to go to Tucson and meet Dr. Schwartz. Because of his academic accomplishments, I felt awkward about calling him anything but Dr. Schwartz. After all, he didn't invest years in obtaining his doctorate for nothing. But he would not allow such formality and insisted that I call him Gary. Besides being modest, he was warm and personable.

As we sat down, Gary began explaining that my timing was interesting because he had lost someone close to him two days before. While Gary was talking I saw a male spirit standing next to him.

"Great!" I thought. "What if he doesn't want to hear from a relative right now?" Sometimes those on the other side can be impatient.

The male spirit pulled out a wrench and started tapping Gary on the head with it. It was so funny I could hardly keep a straight face. I was also trying hard to listen to Gary's words of wisdom. Finally, I couldn't concentrate any longer.

"Gary, there is a man that is with you, either your uncle or your great-uncle. He's not an academic like you. He's holding a wrench in his hand and he's tapping you on the head in a teasing manner. He's mechanical. He works with tools and is good at fixing things. He's a down-to-earth kind of guy."

Gary said, "Yes, that's fine. We'll talk about that after I test you."

I took a deep breath and we continued. Gary was interested in testing me to see whether I could bring through any messages or details about the recently deceased person that he had mentioned earlier. He provided no other information — not age, gender, or circumstance.

After a short pause I said, "I see an old woman. She's petite with white hair and she has a small dog with her." I felt a little unfulfilled, because a lot of old people with little dogs die. I guess I wanted to say that it was a kid with a nose ring or a man wearing a purple polka-dot dress shirt, something unusual. But there are only two genders and many human generalities. It's the little details that define the person and add impact to a reading.

Dr. Schwartz sat silently for a moment and then said, "Go on."

I was really nervous; Dr. Schwartz is Harvard educated and taught at both Harvard and Yale. He is a well-respected scholar and I wanted to exceed his expectations of me. He also works with some of the best-known mediums in the world and I wanted to leave a lasting impression on him. This would not be easy. I was flashed a picture but I didn't want to reveal it, it seemed so insignificant.

Apparently my facial expression betrayed me because Dr. Schwartz encouraged me. "Just say whatever you get. It's okay to be wrong."

"I see a paperboy selling newspapers on a street corner, he's in New York City. He's holding up the newspaper and showing it to me. The person on the other side is saying, 'I do not walk alone.' "

Dr. Schwartz jotted this down.

"Flowers are important to your friend," I added. Dr. Schwartz didn't respond.

I continued, and we carried out the rest of the session while I shared many other personal details.

When the session was over, Dr. Schwartz said, "Let me tell you what your information means."

I couldn't wait to hear. I could have been wrong on the gender, age, and a hundred other things. How nerve-racking! Now was not the time to be wrong.

He started off by telling me that the person who had just died was named Susy Smith and was in fact an old woman. She was eighty-nine, just shy of her ninetieth birthday. They had been colleagues and good friends. She was petite and had white hair, and had once been a newspaper reporter in New York City. And, indeed, she had a little dog she had loved that had died years ago.

The statement "I do not walk alone" was also of significance to Gary. Susy had stated before she died that she hoped she'd be able to walk again on the other side. She had relied heavily on a wheelchair at the time of her death. Susy was letting Gary know that she was whole again. Also, she had always loved children but had had none of her own. I had described her as standing beside a male child. Susy was now taking care of children; she was mothering them. She was letting Gary know that she walks among children on the other side.

The reference to flowers was right on, because Susy used to paint pictures of different types of flowers. There were many other details that let Gary know that she was alive and well on the other side. Gary then gave me feedback concerning the male spirit that stood beside him, the spirit I had commented on earlier.

Gary let me know that he had an uncle who used to joke around with him when he was a child. His uncle had owned a hardware store and was very mechanical. Apparently Gary's uncle is still teasing him from the other side. Confirmation is sweet to a medium; it allows us to share a personal moment with the people we are reading. I feel blessed to meet the colorful spirits who communicate their messages to those who still long for them.

In April 2001 I had another test placed before me. Dr. Schwartz had asked a question of his late friend Susy. He wanted Susy to hear his question and send her answer through any of the mediums participating in his study. We were not allowed to know what the question was and we were all tested independently.

Dr. Schwartz asked me if I knew the answer. (There's some pressure!) I kept getting that it was something that Susy wanted to bequeath to Dr. Schwartz. I repeatedly saw a scene from *The Wizard of Oz* where Dorothy is holding her little dog, Toto, in a handbasket. I described this and Dr. Schwartz asked me to elaborate on what I was seeing.

While Dr. Schwartz was talking to our secretary-recorder about the notes he was taking, I whispered, "Her dog."

His ears perked right up. "What did you say?"

I said, "Her dog. Who has her dog? She wants you to have her dog, she says no one will love her dog like you will."

I continued, and at the end of our session I was told that the question that Dr. Schwartz had asked Susy was, "Who do you want to take your dog?" That's what I refer to as a psychic high-five. Score!

People ask me how I feel about Gary. We have a multifaceted relationship. He is an impressive man and an advanced scientist. I respect his foresight, his humor, and his strength. You get the picture: I really admire him.

Being Gary's research medium has given me great focus with my gift. I had raw ability when I met Gary, but I lacked a frame of reference that would help me push the boundaries of my ability. As a result of my lab testing and the challenges posed to me by Gary, I have become more bold in my readings. There is a big difference between being able to receive the name of a deceased relative and being able to answer a specific question posed to the other side without being privy to the question. I really had to work on being focused to accomplish something at this level of difficulty.

One reason is that a question posed to the deceased and requiring an answer from a lab medium can be seen as a demand on the deceased. It's not necessarily an emotionally based reading, it's academic. A deceased scientist like Susy might be interested in participating, whereas someone else may not. Also, mediums are simply secretaries to the dead. We're just telling you what the deceased says.

Lab readings are different because we are not able to make an emotional connection with the spirit on the other side through their emotional connection to the sitter. When I do a reading, I feel what the spirit feels for my client. I receive memories that connect the two, and images of objects that may bind them. Having both energies physically present (the lost loved one and the sitter) allows me to facilitate a physical connection between the two parties by acting as a medium.

When I'm working for the lab, I often don't even have a sitter in the same state I am in. I am not told the sitter's gender, age, or anything I can connect to. I simply receive information from the other side and pass it on to the lab to be again passed on and graded by the sitter.

Although the result appears to be the same whether a sitter is present or not, I personally am left a bit empty when the sitter isn't there with me. Without knowing that I succeeded in bridging a gap for the sitter, I miss out on the personal connection that occurs when I sit down with a client. However, that's a small price to pay to contribute to science; I hope that by doing this I can help make being a medium better for those who follow me.

Being a research medium is unique; we learn to rely on our information no matter how strange it might seem, and we must share it in order for it to be documented. We have also learned to function under difficult circumstances and on command.

Research mediums tend to be straightforward with our information and sometimes we have to remember to be sensitive. I remind myself with every reading that being honest and sensitive to my client is paramount. Being a research medium has made me stronger and has taught me endless life lessons.

To be able to test my gift means a lot to me. Not only do I gain confidence, I have the opportunity to refine my skills. I do this by taking note of the information I receive, how it comes through, and what it feels like. I look at my psychic and medium information with open eyes. For example, I have learned that those on the other side can bring their messages through only by accessing concepts with which I am already familiar, such as names, pictures, and places. In other words, I have to comprehend it before I can pass it on. So my own life experiences go hand in hand with using my gift.

For example, since I am familiar with law enforcement, especially in the area of homicide, when I bring through a murder victim I can easily receive verdicts and courtroom information on the perpetrator(s). I also have a knack for getting into the mind of a perpetrator. I've noticed John Edward's medical knowledge because he is very good at determining cause of death and medical diagnoses. Mediums have specialties. We have our own strong points and individual style to enhance our abilities. Variety is good.

I was in Tucson one day on business and arranged to meet Gary for dinner at a Mexican restaurant to catch up. The soft glow of the restaurant was easy on the eyes and I was delighted to be in such good company. Joe, Gary, my friend Catherine, and I sat down in a booth for some spicy cuisine.

After we ordered, Gary mentioned that he had a challenge for me. Let me emphasize this was not a lab test, simply an informal challenge.

Gary told me that Susy, his friend on the other side, might be paying visits to a child. This child claimed to see and hear Susy. His question was, "Who's the child and what can you tell me about the child's mother?"

I sat back in my seat and took in the question. "I see a child in the hospital; she has lost her hair."

I gave Gary a name, and I was off on the child's name by one letter. I included other details and messages of love concerning the child.

Gary told us, "The child has cancer, but I'll have to find out if there was hair loss." (There was.)

Next Gary asked, "Where does Susy visit the child?"

"On the child's bed."

Gary said that was correct.

The child I speak of is a feisty, bright light energy. She, too, has the gift and is learning to define it. This is partly why Susy has chosen her to connect with from the other side. She is not only accessible, she is enjoyable.

Gary then asked, "What about the mother?"

"I feel like the mother is a psychic who has been on TV," I replied.

Susy then showed me an image of Stevie Nicks of Fleetwood Mac. I looked at Gary and said, "Laurie Campbell. Is it Laurie Campbell?"

"Are you asking me, or are you telling me?" he asked.

"I am telling you." I had never seen Laurie Campbell before, in person or otherwise. But for some reason, whenever I heard Laurie's name in passing at the lab, I'd see Stevie Nicks in my head. I know it was Susy who had been orchestrating this visual comparison to give me a reference to draw on.

Gary wasn't sure why I associated Stevie Nicks with Laurie (he isn't familiar with Fleetwood Mac), but he said that in fact the mother was Laurie Campbell. I knew nothing personal about Laurie before the challenge except that she's a consistent research medium. Susy accessed the only information that I had stored on Laurie.

Fortunately, it was all that was needed to give Gary his answer. I shared the Stevie Nicks comparison with Laurie Campbell on a later date, when I spoke with her for the first time. Laurie said that she actually had a conversation with Susy before Susy died. In this conversation Laurie had talked to Susy about how she wore dresses similar in style to those Stevie Nicks wears, and how she and Stevie Nicks have other personal similarities.

The information resonated with Laurie and showed me once again that what means nothing to one person can be important to another. Susy spent much of her time and energy on earth trying to prove the existence of life after death. Susy still works to prove her case that human energy continues to exist after death while she walks on the other side.

✦ *"You Have Got to Be Kidding!"*

I have read for many sitters in the name of science. There was one who left the serious Professor Schwartz giggling on the phone. For those of you who don't know Gary, this is out of character for him.

I received a call from Gary at a specified time so that I could read for a test sitter for the lab. The test was set up like a conference call between Gary, the sitter, and me; it was recorded and later transcribed. Both Laurie Campbell and I were utilized (individually) for this test.

The reading went as follows: I was asked what, if anything, I was receiving on the sitter. A barrage of information flooded through and I laid it out neatly for the sitter. The sitter is not allowed to speak to me until I am formally finished giving my information.

I cannot go into great detail about the personal aspects of my sitter's reading, for he is well known and would like his privacy. I knew that he was significant, because I was being told by his late father that his son carries the weight of the world on his shoulders.

Well, that's a lot of responsibility! So I proceeded to advise my sitter on what he needed to do to take care of his health. I shared messages for him from his loved ones and conducted his reading as I would a reading for any regular client. I shared causes of death and personal details about his family members who had passed away, and I was glad to connect.

After we finished, Gary asked, "Do you know whom you just read for?"

I said no.

"Allison, you just read for Deepak Chopra!"

This information was later scored by Dr. Chopra as being approximately 80 percent accurate.

Most of you will know who he is. For those who don't, Deepak Chopra is one of the best-known authors in the world and a very spiritual being. This is funny because I'd just advised a man who is not only wise himself but connected to the very wise. He has published numerous best-selling self-help books. The man advises heads of state, celebrities, royalty, you name it. And here I was helping him!

I told him that I was honored to have read for him. I felt pretty good to be able to give something back to a man who frequently gives so much of himself to others. Some people are givers, some are takers, and most are in between. When a person is mostly a giver, he can deplete himself. When he's mostly a taker, he depletes others. One needs the energy to be returned to have balance. I hoped I had given him something worthwhile. After a few words with Deepak, spoken against the background of Gary's laughter, the test was concluded. I will never forget that reading.

✦ *The Pilot*

While writing this book I was given the opportunity to audition for a television pilot. The producers wanted to sample my talent through a phone reading for one of their executives, named Brian. I usually prefer to read a client in person, so I was a bit leery. The morning of my interview arrived and I prepared for my conference call reading.

My first observation was that there was a tragedy connected to Brian's sister. Her loved one on the other side showed me a car that was significant to her. I stated that the person who passed had died because of an inability to breathe. This was key to Brian, and he confirmed it, so I elaborated further, providing personal details for Brian's sister.

I was able to provide information for his sister that would confirm her deceased friend's presence.

I also told Brian that his sister was going to marry the love of her life. This didn't make sense to Brian, because his sister was in a less than ideal relationship. A month after the reading, she attended her class reunion and began dating a former classmate. They made plans to be married in October 2002.

Brian's grandfather then came through and spoke of an accordion. Brian said that his grandmother and brother both play the accordion. I liked this object because it's not a common household item; it's unusual. Something unusual is always more compelling to the sitter. The good thing about having a conference call was that whenever Brian's jaw dropped, his coworker Debbie would laugh and keep the atmosphere light.

After I hung up, my husband asked how it went. It was a solid reading. I was satisfied. I told Joe that I knew I would be asked to read for another executive. Sure enough, the next week I received an invitation to read for Karen, who works with Kelsey Grammar as the vice president of TV development for Grammnet. Another phone reading. Aaarghh! But would I pass it up? Never!

A week later I received the call from Karen. She was vivacious and pleasant. I connected with a friend of hers on the other side. He described the small town where they grew up, and also described Karen's childhood home, both inside and out, where they used to play. Her friend also illustrated a rope-and-board swing that hung from a tree.

The reading went well, but I didn't feel I was deserving of my nickname, the Cosmic Two-by-Four — used purely in jest, of course. I am accustomed to giving information that stuns people. Sometimes I am my own worst critic. But toward the end of her reading, I was shown Bugs Bunny and WB. I asked her if she used to work for Warner Brothers.

She was shocked. "Yes!" she said. "I not only worked there, but I have a meeting there tomorrow." This would be her first return visit since she had stopped working for WB. The timing had a great impact on her reading.

I then asked about the trip to Europe that she was either about to take or had just taken. She confirmed this, too. She was currently preparing for a European trip. I connected with my sitter and she couldn't have been more pleased with her reading.

I was asked to come out to LA to audition for the show. More than a hundred gifted people had originally been considered, and I was one of the eighteen selected to audition in front of the cameras at Paramount. We would be vying for one of five different positions.

I was the first to audition. I read for three different sitters, and all went well. I loved being on the Paramount Studios lot; there is so much history there. The rest of the auditions took place over the next two days, while I did some sightseeing with my new-found friends and we talked of the enormous pressures of showbiz.

That afternoon, the two women I had grown really fond of found out they were being sent home. We had one last night out together. Five of us decided to go out for a nice dinner. My companions included Penny Thornton, aka Duchess, who'd been Princess Diana's astrologer and adviser for six years; Ulrich Bold, an evolutionary astrologer; Freya, who specializes in runes; and Joann, a medium like me. We had a marvelous dinner and stayed up late talking like kids at a slumber party. But we were adults who had to get up in the morning, so eventually we called it a night. I made some special friends on my trip to LA, ones I'll always be grateful for having.

When the dust settled, I was one of the five left standing. Filming the pilot for the show was an experience I will never forget. I loved working with other people in my field who had talents unfamiliar to me. Every single person on that set taught me something about myself.

Taping the *Oracles* pilot turned out to be one of many serendipitous occurrences that helped to bring me where I am today. I was able to see that people in every profession disagree from time to time on what the right way of doing things is and that that's okay. I learned how to set my personal boundaries in a profession that I knew very little about. I realized I cared greatly about these strangers around me who had lost people they loved. I did not want to get away from them; I wanted to be a part of their healing. Every lesson learned brought me a step closer to becoming who I had been all along, a medium.

About the Author

Allison DuBois's unique story, the inspiration of the hit NBC TV show *Medium*, started during her final semester at the Arizona State University, while she was an intern at the district attorney's office. Soon after, researchers at the University of Arizona documented her ability through a series of tests in which she scored exceptionally high on accuracy and specificity. This validation persuaded Allison to become a professional medium and profiler instead of a prosecuting attorney.

In her short career, Allison has conducted over 1,200 personal readings. In those readings, she helps to ease the pain people feel from losing a loved one. She continues to support the use of science to investigate the afterlife. She has spent the last four years participating in various tests for the University of Arizona. Allison takes an active role in the direction and execution of research as a member of the Veritas Research Program Mediums Committee and is a member of the Medium Advisory Board for the Forever Family Foundation.

Allison donates her time to missing and murdered persons and criminal cases for agencies across the country. She is contacted by law enforcement agencies and families to help find missing and murdered people. Allison also assists in jury selection for district attorney's offices. Each of these is a means for her to give back to the world for being so blessed.

Allison maintains close ties to the show *Medium* as a consultant.